# More Than a
# Father

*Breaking Down
The Barriers
to Intimacy With God*

# Duane Rawlins

Emerald
Books

P.O. Box 635
Lynnwood, Washington 98046

MORE THAN A FATHER

ISBN 1-883002-00-1

Printed in the United States of America

# Contents

# *Acknowledgment*

*I* am grateful to my friend and colleague, Groff Benge for his tremendous help and editorial skills. Without Geoff I could never have conceived and created this book. My son, Matthew was also very helpful in critiquing and forming questions to be answered at the end of each chapter. My wife, Lee Ann, constantly encouraged me to hang in there and finish the book. Without the many friends who taught me these principles, I would have little to say.

# *About the Author*

$D$r. M. Duane Rawlins, is an educator, businessman, speaker, and father. He received his doctorate in Education from UCLA and spent 25 years working in the public school system of southern California where his last assignment was the Ass't Superintendent of schools, in Simi Valley. In 1972, he moved to Salem, OR. with his wife Betty, and their three children and became President of Rawlins Realty. He has been actively involved with missions and the local church for most of his life. Facing the personal challenges of loosing his wife and oldest son to illness has only deepened his desire for intimacy with His Heavenly Father. thankful for the opportunity to share this message of the Father's heart of love, he travels internationally bringing hope and healing to many. In 1986, God faithfully provided a new helpmate and wife, Lee Ann, who travels and teaches along side of Duane. Between them, they gave 6 children and 11 grandchildren. They reside in Salem, OR.

# PREFACE

Knowing God is the privilege of all Christians. There is no greater joy and pleasure in all the universe than to travel a lifetime in intimate fellowship and relationship with the creator of the uni-verse. Today, however, many Christians do not enjoy this close intimacy with God. Instead, they have confined God to the rituals of the Sunday church service, and when they feel the need to spend time with Him, that is where they go.

God is not confined to our churches and rituals, however. He is boundless and endless. He created the universe and all that is in it, and He waits patiently to enter into close intimate relationship with every Christian. He has already taken the first steps toward us, sending His Son into the world to make a way for us to be reconciled to Him. Now He waits with open arms for us to move towards Him.

Moving towards God and entering into close relationship with Him require more than just acceptance of Jesus as our Lord and Savior. They require a life-long commitment to make Jesus number one in our lives, to do His will, and to daily seek Him and spend time with Him.

How to move into an intimate relationship with God is the subject of this book. The book first lays out those things that hold us back from entering into the kind of relationship God wants to enjoy with us. It then offers practical advice on how to overcome those obstacles. Not the final or definitive word on everything pertaining to knowing God, the book sets forth some principles for those who want to know God more intimately. The principles are tried and true, worked out in my life and the lives of those I have come into contact with throughout my years as a Christian. Humbly I present them to you so that you may truly know God.

Chapter One

# *SEVEN AREAS*
# *OF STRUGGLE*

*T*he New Testament declares that as Christians we are the bride of Christ. This description denotes the special relationship God wants to have with us. When a man chooses a bride, he is choosing a woman with whom to enter into the most intimate of all human relationships. So too with God: He has chosen us, His church, to be His bride and to enter into close intimacy with Him.

Many Christians, unfortunately, never experience the joy and pleasure of this close relationship. Instead of experiencing closeness and intimacy with God, they experience frustration and guilt as they struggle along in their Christian lives. We all struggle at times, but by no means are struggles, frustrations, and guilt to be the testimony of a relationship with God. For this reason, let's begin by examining seven areas in which Christians will struggle when they fail to experience closeness and intimacy with God.

## Difficulty in Understanding the Ways of God

> *Oh, the depth of the riches of the wisdom and knowledge of God! How unsearchable his judgments, and his paths beyond tracing out!* (Romans 11:33)

> *"For my thoughts are not your thoughts, neither are your ways my ways,"* declares the LORD. *"As the heavens are higher than the earth, so are my ways higher than your ways and my thoughts than your thoughts"* (Isaiah 55:8-9).

We can study the Bible and attend Bible college or seminary and learn a lot about God and about theology. But knowing a lot about a person is very different from knowing the person. I do not personally know the president of the United States, but I know a great deal about him. His life is put under the microscope daily by the media, and in the process we learn much about the president. Yet all I have read and know about the president is no substitute for knowing him. I cannot walk into the Oval Office at the White House and say, "Hi, Mr. President, let's spend some time together." Only a few people have that privilege, and I am not one of them.

I may know all the president's likes and dislikes, his idiosyncrasies, the way he likes to do things, the things that anger him, the things that please him. However, I can never understand why, for example, he likes some things and dislikes others unless I enter into a personal relationship with him. Then, during our times together he tell me his reasons for liking or disliking particular things. He can explain why he does some things a certain way and why some things anger him while others amuse him. I then pass from knowing *about* him to knowing and understanding *him*. I come to understand his motivations behind what he does, and I can appreciate hime more fully.

So, too, with God. We can know all there is to know about Him, but such knowledge is no substitute for having a personal and intimate relationship with Him. The verses from Romans and Isaiah point out that God's ways and judgments are unsearchable and unfathomable—higher than our human thoughts and ways of doing things. We could spend an eternity trying to understand them, but we will find that understanding only if God chooses to give it to us. The place that God chooses to reveal such knowledge to us is within the bonds of intimate relationship. Once we enter into that relationship with God, we can better know and understand His ways.

These days we see a great deal of theological saber rattling. Having devoted their lives to studying the Bible as a way to understand God, many Christians are locked in mortal combat with others who have done the same but have drawn different conclusions about the nature and character of God. They struggle, each trying to prove that he or she is right and the other is wrong. The end result is pride, arrogance, hurt, and bitterness. However, knowing and understanding the ways of God bring humility as we see how little we really know and understand about God.

A number of years ago when I was a schoolteacher, there was much concern about the possibility of a nuclear war, so much so that we had emergency nuclear attack drills at school, the aim of which was to teach students what they needed to do in case of a nuclear attack. Students were instructed that at the sound of the word *drop* they were to immediately stop whatever they were doing and fall to the floor, where they were to pull themselves into a tight ball. Whenever we had our drill, that is exactly what the students would do. Regardless of what they were doing, they would drop to the floor and curl into a ball. We Christians need to develop the same kind of reflex. In the presence of God we should be skinning our knees to get to the ground in humility before Him, since humility is the key to understanding the ways of

God and leads to intimacy and fellowship with
God.

## An Inability to Develop a Real
## and Lasting Relationship with God

Christianity involves relationship with the
Lord. Unfortunately, today such a relationship
has often been usurped by a set of rules that
encompass everything from our daily behavior
to what clothes are appropriate for church and
the form our church worship should take. Often
the rules are well intentioned—even necessary—
but they are no substitute for knowing God. All
too often, though, a substitute is what they become. If we will only keep this rule and that rule,
we will have a relationship with God. Nothing
could be further from the truth. We do not develop an intimate relationship with God by keeping rules. All we manage to do is demonstrate
that we are compliant.

The Bible does, of course, contain rules and
laws, which are important but not a substitute for our
personal relationship with the Father, the Son, and
the Holy Spirit. Knowing God personally through
intimate relationship allows us to go beyond the
facade of rule keeping and to enter into the core of
Christianity.

## Difficulty in Worshipping God

*"Yet a time is coming and has now come when the*

*true worshipers will worship the Father in spirit
and truth, for they are the kind of worshipers the
Father seeks. God is spirit, and his worshipers must
worship in spirit and in truth"* (John 4:23-24).

To worship God basically means to tell God
the truth about Himself. Since worship is centered
in truth, once we know the truth about God—that
He loves us, that He sent His Son to die for us, and
that daily He cares for us—we can begin to enter
into worship. The worship Jesus is speaking of in
these verses from John's gospel is worship that
comes not from knowing about God but from
knowing God in a real and personal way—worship that grows out of understanding the ways of
God and not from simply having a lot of information about God. If we want to be a true worshiper
in the way Jesus spoke of, we must enter into an
intimate relationship with God. Only then will we
be truly able to worship God in spirit and in truth.

## Difficulty in Relating God
## to Our Daily Living

Information alone does not have the power
to move us to do something about the information. We may be shocked and horrified by certain
information, thrilled and delighted by other information, but in and of itself, information is
fairly neutral. We can accept it, or we can reject it,
but it doesn't compel us to do anything else about
it. Before we are moved to act on certain informa-

tion, an overriding compulsion must come to our hearts that the information is right and that we must embrace it and act upon it. The kind of compulsion that leads a person to surrender his or her life to the Lord upon hearing the gospel, we call conviction.

If most of our experience with God is based on having information about Him, we will find it difficult to relate God to our everyday life. God will be to us an intellectual concept at odds with today's world. When God tells us that we should love our neighbors as ourselves, we will find it hard to do so because we will have no real motivating force. We will not have personally experienced God's love for us as undeserving sinners. Experiencing God's love, however, soon moves us to love our neighbors as ourselves and the experience becomes an important part of our daily life. Having experienced God's undeserved love, we are compelled to reach out in love to those around us, and we then find it easy to relate God to our everyday life.

## Ashamed of Our Faith

> *"If anyone is ashamed of me and my words in this adulterous and sinful generation, the Son of Man will be ashamed of him when he comes in his Father's glory with the holy angels"* (Mark 8:38).

Throughout history, few people have gone to their death for what they thought was a good idea.

Those who have died or have been executed for their ideas have been convinced beyond any shadow of a doubt that they were right. One need only to read the history of the early church to learn of people who were totally convinced as to the veracity of the gospel. As a result, these people went willingly to their death, often in very brutal and gruesome ways. They did not willingly go to their death because they thought the gospel was a good idea. Rather, they knew God, and they had a daily relationship with Him, and because they did they knew the gospel to be true and were not ashamed of it—even if it meant their death.

Today, in some parts of the world, Christians are still persecuted and put to death. Such things are unlikely to happen to most Western Christians, however. Yet the principle is the same: we must be convinced in our heart that the gospel is right before we will ever stand up unashamedly for it. If we think the gospel is only a good idea, if we have the information in our head but are not fully convinced in our heart, we will have difficulty standing up for the gospel when the time comes for us to do so.

As Christians, we need the strength of character that allows us to stand firm when others stumble, and to speak up when others are silent. We need the strength of character that shows God we are not at all ashamed of Him but rather are convinced of the truth of His word and are willing to do whatever it takes to share His word with others. This kind of strength comes only through a close relationship with God.

## Tendency Towards Legalism

*For I can testify about them that they are zealous for God, but their zeal is not based on knowledge* (Romans 10:2).

Some of the most zealous people I have met are people bound by legalism. Their zealousness is aimed at getting other people to keep the same rules they keep, since these people believe their rules are the right rules and the only ones worth keeping. Such zealousness usually leads to bitterness and faction fighting over whose rules are the right ones. But Christianity, as we have already discussed, consists not of keeping rules but of living in daily communion with God. Legalism is a poor substitute for intimacy with God. Intimate relationship with God brings freedom to one's daily life, while rule keeping only leads to bondage and frustration at the inability to keep the rules.

## Drifting Away from God

*But I am afraid that just as Eve was deceived by the serpent's cunning, your minds may somehow be led astray from your sincere and pure devotion to Christ* (2 Corinthians 11:3).

When we have no personal intimacy with God, human grit and determination are simply not enough to sustain us in our Christian life. Over time we begin to drift away from God. We often make excuses for our drifting away and tell ourselves it really doesn't matter, since God doesn't care about our needs anyway. Nothing could be further from the truth. God does care about us, and He longs to meet our needs. We, however, seem to lack the desire to really know God and be with Him. It's the same kind of desire we experience when we fall in love. All we want is to be with the other person. No matter what the time of day or night, we just want to be with the other person. A similar desire is necessary to sustain a lasting and close relationship with God. Once we have experienced true intimacy with Him, we begin to see how personally He takes care of us.

## Personal Application Points

1) Do you find yourself struggling in any of the areas discussed?

2) If so, why do you think you have struggled in the particular area?

3) Are there some positive steps you can take to overcome this?

Chapter Two

# *KNOWING GOD*

Knowing God is the most important thing anyone can do in life. In his letter to the Philippians, the apostle Paul says, "I want to know Christ and the power of his resurrection and the fellowship of sharing in his sufferings, becoming like him in his death, and so, somehow, to attain to the resurrection from the dead" (3:10-11). Earlier in the same chapter of Philippians, Paul lists his "credentials": circumcised on the eighth day, an Israelite from the tribe of Benjamin, a Pharisee who zealously persecuted the early church, a Hebrew of Hebrews (verses 4-6)—an impressive list of credentials in Paul's day.

Like Paul, many of us have a list of credentials which are basically a record of our successes. We may have undergone specialized training for a certain job or skill or we may have earned a college degree. Perhaps we are wise and gifted in certain areas. Or possibly we were born into an important or famous family. These are our credentials, and rightly or wrongly, society uses them to measure us.

Paul had his credentials, but he told us that the most important thing in his life was not his credentials but knowing Christ and being wholly identified with Him. He tells us that of all the knowledge he has gained throughout his life— and it was considerable—none of it compared to the joy of knowing Christ and being fully and totally identified with Him. Even today, despite all the vast areas of knowledge and learning we have open to us, nothing compares to the joy and fulfillment that comes from knowing Christ in an intimate and personal way.

In Genesis 1:26-27 we read: "Then God said, 'Let us make man in our image, in our likeness'.... So God created man in his own image, in the image of God he created him; male and female he created them." Of course, the question here is, *Why* did God create us? Of all the philosophical and theological questions man has attempted to answer through the ages, this is the most discussed. In times past, such great philosophers and thinkers as Plato, Aristotle, and Voltaire have attempted to answer this question.

Since so many great men have sought to answer the question, it is important to ask which great man is the most eminently qualified to answer the age-old question. The answer is found in Jesus Christ. In prayer with His Father, Jesus says, "Now this is eternal life [or this is the answer to life's greatest question]: *that they may know you*, the only true God, and Jesus Christ, whom you have sent" (John 17:3, emphasis added).

In this passage, the word rendered "know" means more than we English speakers would normally think. In the classical Greek language—which the New Testament was originally written in—there are two words for knowing: *gnosis* and *epignosis*. Gnosis has to do with head knowledge, with understanding information and data; epignosis, with experiential, intimate heart knowledge. It's the kind of knowing that leads to intimacy between a husband and wife. In Genesis 4:1 we read, "And Adam knew Eve his wife; and she conceived, and bare Cain" (KJV). It's the same word. It's also the same word Paul uses when he encourages us to know God. Paul is speaking about knowing God intimately, about having intimacy with God just as a man has intimacy with his wife. Since it is not enough to just know about God, we must know Him in an intimate and personal way, since God created us to have intimate relationship with us.

The apostle Paul prayed for the believers at Ephesus: "I keep asking that the God of our Lord Jesus Christ, the glorious Father, may give you the

Spirit of wisdom and revelation, so that you may know him better" (Ephesians 1:17). Later in the same letter, Paul encourages the Ephesians to "approach God with freedom and confidence" (Ephesians 3:12), because freedom and confidence are the direct outgrowth of an intimate relationship with God.

Daniel tells us, "but the people that do know [*epignosis*—intimately know] their God shall be strong and do *exploits*" (Daniel 11:32, KJV). If you feel weak but want to do things for God that count, get to know Him better. However, in desiring to do things for God and to see miracles happen in your daily life, be careful that not to get so caught up in things that you lose sight of your relationship with God. It can happen. Matthew 7:22 tells us about Christians who get so caught up with the gift that they forget the giver. In the passage, Jesus talks about the people who will come to Him on the day of judgement boasting of how they have healed the sick, raised the dead, and done many other miracles. In verse 23, Jesus tells us He will say to them, "I never knew [*epignosis*—intimately knew] you. Away from me, you evildoers!" In other words, Jesus is saying, "You knew a lot *about* me and how do to things in My name, but you never took the time to enter into a personal, intimate relationship with Me. Therefore, there is no room for you in My kingdom among those who did know Me intimately and personally."

It is challenging to think that we can work

miracles and do many mighty things in Jesus' name yet still not know the Lord. We must therefore be ever careful that we do know Him and that everything we do as Christians flows from the intimate relationship we enjoy with Him.

If our desire is to live the Christian life to the fullest, we should take note of the words of Peter:

> *Do you want more and more of God's kindness and peace? Then learn to know him better and better. For as you know him better, he will give you, through his great power, everything you need for living a truly good life: he even shares his own glory and his own goodness with us!* (2 Peter 1:2-3, TLB)

## Personal Application Points

1) What are your credentials?

2) How important are your credentials to you?

3) Is your knowledge of God based on information about Him or on intimate experiential knowledge of Him?

# Chapter Three

# *EASTERN AND WESTERN CHURCH CONCEPTS OF GOD*

$A$s anyone who has studied church history knows, there are two main branches of Christianity: Eastern, or Orthodox, Christianity and Western Christianity.

Around A.D. 200, lawyer and Christian leader Tertullian began to fashion what has become the Western Christian view of God. Tertullian saw God as a legislator and judge and emphasized man's moral responsibility rather than the mercy of God.

For Tertullian, good works were the appropriate payment for penalties imposed upon us by God because of our guilt. Before Tertullian, such thoughts were unheard of and are still not part of Eastern Christian thought today.

The difference between the two branches of Christianity became very real to me one day as I sat in a class in Kona, Hawaii, listening to Dr. Frost teach about the father heart of God. As he spoke, I began to see how much my background and conservative Christian experience had caused me to be totally Western in my approach to God. I realized I was out of balance. I needed to see more of God's grace, humility, flexibility, forgivenss, compassion, and mercy. I had always looked at things from the other side. I thought that true Christianity should be rational, structured, and responsible. I needed to embrace more of the view of Christianity held by the Eastern Church.

The figure in table one compares the emphases of the Eastern and Western churches.

It is good to look at the different emphases in this manner and see where our thinking and understanding of God fit. In speaking about the Eastern and Western branches of Christianity, I don't mean to imply that one is right and the other wrong. Both are, in a sense, right, and I believe that every Christian needs both of these understandings of God. Western Christian thinking is based on rationality: things have to be logical and make sense. Eastern Christian thinking, by contrast, is mystical and postulates that things about God are beyond knowing. Talk of God is mystical talk that we can never fully understand. Western Christian thinking is structured and emphasizes merits, while Eastern Christian thought is flexible and emphasizes God's mercy.

| Western | Eastern |
| --- | --- |
| Rational | Mystical |
| Based on dogma | Emphasizes humility |
| Structured | Flexible |
| Emphasizes man's responsibility | Emphasizes God's sovereignty |
| Emphasizes man's merits | Emphasizes God's mercy |

**Figure 1**

According to Western thinking, salvation is a plan. First you confess, then you repent, then you are baptized, and finally you are added to the church. In Eastern thinking, salvation happens. Why it happens is beyond understanding. God just does it.

Western Christian thought is based on dogma and emphasizes man's responsibility, while Eastern Christian thought emphasizes humility and the sovereignty of God. In the Eastern Christian sphere, you just know that God is at work. You don't know how He works or why He works; He is sovereign, and you simply know He is at work. In the Western Christian sphere, the Word of God is viewed as a do-it-yourself kit to be memorized and applied to daily life.

As I alluded earlier, what every Christian needs is an amalgam of both forms of thinking. Neither Western nor Eastern Christian thinking, on its own, provides the full understanding of God. Put together, the two forms of thought provide a rich understanding of the nature and character of God.

If we adhere blindly to one or the other of these forms of thinking, we become victims of theological extremes. Rigorous adherence to the Eastern form of thought leads to irresponsibility, while rigorous adherence to Western thought forms leads to condemnation and fear. Such extremes, of course, play right into Satan's hand. Satan wants to push Christians to extremes in their understanding of God and destroy the common ground of love and unity among Christians.

The chart in figure two summarizes the different understandings of God these two forms of Christian thought hold.

God created the law, and the law is important. However, God is also the author of grace. He is our judge and will ultimately judge each of us, but He will judge us as a father judges his children. He is legislator and executioner, but He is also our redeemer. All too often we respond to God and his law out of fear. We need to see God as our redeemer, merciful and forgiving. When we see Him this way, we will be moved to respond to Him with love.

| Western | Emphasis | Eastern |
|---|---|---|
| Law | *Emphasis* | Grace |
| Judge | *God is* | Father |
| Legislator & executioner | *He functions as* | Redeemer |
| Condemnation & punishment | *Who delivers* | Mercy & forgiveness |
| Sinner | *To me a* | Sinner |
| Fear | *Who responds in* | Love |

**Figure 2**

I became a Christian because of a fear of punishment and hell and not because of any great appreciation for God's mercy and forgiveness. I viewed God almost exclusively from the Western Christian viewpoint, and it was a number of years before I began to understand that God was also my father and loved me as His child. This understanding revolutionized my Christian life and walk.

If we lean too heavily on the Western Christian view, we must make every effort to see and understand the Eastern Christian view. If, however, the Eastern view is all we know, we need to understand the Western view that there is a law and God is a judge, that there is conviction and condemnation, and that failure to obey and submit to God brings punishment.

Having a full understanding of who God is will help us avoid the pitfalls of extreme preconceptions about Him, such as those examined in the next two chapters. Such preconceptions cut off intimacy with God rather than encourage it, since they present an inaccurate picture of God, a picture based on partial truth. Since the picture is only partially true, it presents a God who is too harsh, too controlling, too uncaring, or too distant for us to want to enter into intimate relationship with Him. Unfortunately, in the church today, many extreme views of God abound. More than ever, Christians need to grasp the full picture of who God is as presented in both the Eastern and the Western branches of the faith.

## Personal Application Points

1) Which aspects of Eastern or Western Christianity can you identify with, and why?

2) Are there aspects that you feel will add new dimensions to your understanding of God?

3) What are some practical ways you can incorporate the Eastern or Western branch of Christianity into your life?

Chapter Four

# *SOME COMMON MISCONCEPTIONS*

**O**ur greatest hindrance to knowing God intimately is the preconceived ideas we have about who God really is. Each of us has built-in prejudices and misconceptions that filter out those things we don't want to hear or understand. Such a filtering process leads us to the place where everything we believe is in accordance with our prejudices and misconceptions.

To elaborate on this process, let's look at persons A, B and C. Person A has an A filter, person B a B filter, and person C a C filter. These filters could be each person's church background, cultural and ethnic origin, socioeconomic grouping, or any number of circumstances that helped shape and mold these people's personalities. These three people read the Bible and then discuss what they have read. Person A says, "God is wicked and vengeful. All He seems interested in is zapping people." Person B says, "No, that's not true at all. God's a nice person who'll watch out for you." Person C says, "Come on you two, you're both only partly right. God is vengeful sometimes and nice at other times. The secret is to stay on his good side." The three people discuss the matter further and find that they cannot agree on what they have read. Each believes that the conclusion he has drawn about God is the right one and that the other two are simply wrong. None of them considers that there could be even more ideas of who God is.

These people came to such different conclusions because each approached the Bible with his own preconceptions thourgh which he sifted what he was reading. Thus, each reached a different understanding about what he had read. Each had a different filter, and each person's filter altered the person's perception of God.

We all have our own mental filtering system. The forces that have shaped us to be the person we are have also deposited within us a filtering system through which we sift everything we experience. The challenge for us as Christians wanting to know God intimately is to be able to lay aside, as much as possible, our filtering system and its preconceived notions of who God is. When we open ourselves to see God from a different perspective, we are then in a position to know God as he truly is.

This and the following chapter look at some preconceived notions people have about God. Simply because something is a preconception does not, however, mean it is entirely wrong. Indeed, within each of the preconceptions discussed here there are elements of truth about the nature and character of God. Problems arise when truth is mixed in with misunderstanding and error. Satan would like nothing better than for us to blindly and wholeheartedly endorse these concepts. When we do that, we rob ourselves of the full understanding of God and the joy of entering into close communion with Him.

Our preconceptions of God are distorted pictures of God. And a distorted picture is no picture at all. Examining the distortions will give us a clear understanding of what God is *not* like. By seeing what God is not like, we can begin to see what He *is* like.

## COMMON MISCONCEPTIONS

### *God Is Not a Policeman or the Nagging Voice of Our Conscience*

Often people conceive of God as the nagging voice that speaks from their conscience whenever they knowingly and willfully do something wrong—the voice that makes them feel bad about what they did until they either rectify it or manage to silence the voice. When God is thought of in this way, He becomes a policeman waiting for a person to step out of line so that He can haul in and correct the person.

A conscience is valuable, but the truth is that it isn't God's voice at all. It's just our conscience, and our conscience is not infallible. We can harden our conscience by repeated sin, and we can also oversensitize it to the point where things that are not sin can call forth the voice of guilt.

I hardened my conscience once to driving over the speed limit. I managed to readjust my conscience to a 62 mile-per-hour speed limit. Why 62 miles per hour? Because I didn't want to get a ticket and had fairly good reason to believe that the highway patrol would not stop me for speeding if I was traveling at 62 miles per hour. My conscience had become conditioned to the point where it was no longer reliable with regard to driving at the speed limit.

Similarly, we can harden our conscience to more serious moral issues until we can enter into sin without a word from our conscience. Years of wrong conditioning can alter drastically the accuracy of our conscience, causing it to become a very inaccurate and fallible instrument.

Today's media bombard us with all kinds of propaganda that tells us that there are no moral standards, so it's okay to be macho, be mean, be cruel to your wife, be unfaithful, whatever it is, just do it. In the face of such an onslaught, the consciences of many people have become hardened and impaired or have ceased to function at all. To be in such a place is very dangerous. During World War II, many Nazis suffered no violation of their consciences as they hated, persecuted, and annihilated millions of innocent people.

Just as we can harden our conscience, we can also soften and oversensitize it to the point where it is of little use. A workaholic constantly feels guilty (I know, I have been one). When he comes home from work, he begins to think, "I'm so ashamed, I left work fifteen minutes early." It doesn't matter to him that he arrived at work two hours early. Whatever a workaholic does during the day is never quite enough; there's always more to be done. The workaholic begins to hear the nagging voice of guilt in his conscience over leaving work at the end of the day. His conscience has become oversensitized to the point of being self-destructive.

Properly conditioned, our conscience will reflect God's moral and ethical standards. That still doesn't mean our conscience is God's voice. Unless we are aware of this, every time we hear a voice in our conscience we will assume it to be the voice of God. What the voice says to us may be in line with God's moral standard regarding a matter, but that doesn't make it the voice of God.

The danger of equating God with our conscience is this: how can we love, worship, and develop an intimate relationship with someone who points out only our negative attributes? How can we love a God whom we view as a policeman, always waiting for us to step out of line so that he can move in and nail us? Such notions do not seem to be solid enough ground on which to build a lasting and intimate relationship with God.

### God Is Not a "Grand Old Man"

The child's view of God is God as an old man. Many adults have holdovers from the way they were taught to think about God in Sunday school. Try imagining the God of the universe as a thirty-year-old. People have great difficulty thinking of God that way. It seems to us that God ought to be very old, since everything we have ever seen in our lives grows old with the passage of time. God is eternal: He has lived from ages past and will live on eternally into the future. So, we reason, He must be very old. Indeed, virtually every picture painted of God pictures Him as an old man with long white hair and dressed in flowing robes. Despite what human reason tells us, God is not an old man.

Many of us have grown up thinking of God not only as old but also as a bit old-fashioned. When I was growing up, my dad spoke to God in King James English. He would speak quite normally in everyday English until it came time to pray. Then he would wax eloquent in his best King James English. "O Thou who art the most high, we beseech thee this day that thou wouldst draw nigh o us...." And on he would go, as if God were so old and out of touch with the modern world that He couldn't understand everyday modern English. I don't mean to put down my father's sincerity when he prayed. My father was very sincere, and he loved the Lord. I am simply trying to illustrate how this concept of God affects even the way we talk to Him. Indeed, I think God must be very amused by the unnatural and contorted speech we often use when talking to Him.

People today need to see that God is alive and vibrant and vitally interested in them. They need to see that He understands today's world, that He is relevant and contemporary. Given the increasing pressures that society puts upon people today—especially in Western society—people need to know that there is someone who understands those pressures and can help them bear them. To such a person people can relate; they most certainly cannot relate to a "grand old man" in the sky.

### God Is Not Meek and Mild

The notion of God as meek and mild is also a throwback to our Sunday school days when we were taught to pray, "Gentle Jesus, meek and mild." Jesus was meek, if meekness is taken to mean totally selfless, humble, and devoted to righteousness. Today, however, the word meek carries with it an insipid connotation that detracts from and distorts its true meaning. Jesus was definitely not meek by today's measure of the word. The things He did while on earth show His great character, strength, and understanding.

And Jesus was certainly not mild. I don't think anybody who came in contact with Jesus during His time on earth would have drawn the conclusion that He was a mild man. Can we equate mildness with a person who called the religious leaders of the day hypocrites and white-washed tombs; who, when confronted by a seething crowd after He had called Himself the Son of God, walked right through the crowed untouched; who had thousands of people following Him to hear what He had to say and see the miracles He performed; who in anger physically threw the money changers out of the temple; who went deliberately to His death in obedience to His Father's wishes? I don't think any such person could be called mild.

The meek-and-mild concept of God leaves us with a sickly sweet God who has little relevance to the realities of life. This notion of God also distorts the concept of love. God is love, yes, but the kind of love we are presented with in this concept of Jesus as meek and mild is sentimental, and sentimentality is not what the Bible implies when it says God is love.

## God Is Not a Perfectionist

Although it is true that God is perfect, it does not automatically follow that He is a perfectionist. The perfectionist concept of God grows from a misunderstanding of the word *perfect*. Jesus did say, "Be perfect, therefore, as your heavenly Father is perfect" (Matthew 5:48). In all truth, however, we cannot be perfect as God is perfect, because we are not God. A quick look at a dictionary will show that the word *perfect* has a wide range of meanings. The meaning most commonly attributed to "perfect" as it is used today would describe something as exact, faultless, precise, and not deficient in any area. So when we say that something we or someone else has made is perfect, we are really saying that the thing meets our standard for faultlessness. To us the object is exact and precise and therefore perfect. This use of the word leads to the perfectionist concept of God, where we believe that everything we do must be exact and faultless, since God is perfect and expects the same from us.

We reason that since God's standard of perfection is so much higher than ours, our life quickly falls into a cycle of doing things hoping they will be perfect enough for God to accept. This, however, is not what Jesus had in mind when He told us to be perfect. He was not talking about doing something to a certain standard of exactness and faultlessness. He was talking about being. The Greek word translated "perfect" that Jesus used was teleios, which carries the meaning of being complete and mature. Indeed, newer translations of the Bible, such as the New International Version, translate teleios as mature on a number of occasions: Ephesians 4:13; Philippians 3:15; Colossians 4:12; James 1:4. Thus, what Jesus is saying is, "Be mature and complete just as your heavenly Father is mature and complete."

Being mature and complete as the Father is mature and complete basically means that in accordance with all the knowledge and understanding that God possesses—and the Bible tells us that He possesses infinite wisdom and knowledge—God is mature and complete. In the same way that the Father is mature and complete according to the wisdom and knowledge He possesses, we, too, are to be mature and complete in accordance with the wisdom and knowledge *we* possess. Or put more simply, we are to live according to all the spiritual knowledge we possess.

Our lives are a spiritual journey. Every day we learn more about God and how He wants us to live, and every day we have a new challenge to live up to. Living up to all that we know to be true about God at a particular point in time is what it means to be perfect as our heavenly Father is perfect.

It is important to note that God holds us accountable only for the spiritual knowledge we possess and not for what we do not know. Daily our lives should be shining brighter and brighter with the character of God as we live up to the revealed spiritual knowledge we have gained.

Living life under the perfectionist concept of God, wherein we are always trying to do everything exactly and faultlessly for God, soon leads to burnout, condemnation and a lack of joy in the Christian life. But "there is now no condemnation for those who are in Christ Jesus" (Romans 8:1). So if condemnation is the end result of our living the Christian life, most assuredly we are not living our life in the way God intends us to live and enjoy it.

The New Testament books of James and Romans talk about the daily struggle between the flesh and the Spirit that all Christians experience as they attempt to live according to the truth they have. There is no such struggle in God. We are carnal; He is not. We are tempted; He is not. There is nothing in Him that is not light and good and wonderful. He is perfect; we are not. All God asks is that we live our lives according to our knowledge and understanding.

### God Is Not a Spoil-Sport

No one can love, admire, and worship a God whose very existence is viewed negatively. No one wants to be in close relationship with a person he conceives of as only wanting to spoil any enjoyment he may find in life. The very concept of a negative spoil-sport God is at odds with God as revealed in the Bible.

The idea that God is a spoil-sport is a holdover from earlier centuries when God was conceived of as having no joy, no vitality, and no color. Under this concept, God was as an all-seeing eye in the sky, always watching for people who looked overly happy or seemed to be deriving too much enjoyment from life. When He found such people, He moved to bring them back within the bounds of circumspection to the things that were considered "holy" and "Christian." For the Christian caught by this misconception, a stern, dower look at all times was the mark of holiness. There was no room for enjoyment, the world was a serious place, and God was a serious person, and if you were to be like Him, you needed to be serious, too.

Unfortunately, not much has changed today. This concept is still alive and well and more pervasive than we may think, especially among fundamentalist groups. It is kept alive in the idea that if God calls us to do something, it will not be to do something we enjoy or are naturally good at. If we are a gifted musician, God will probably call us to build hospitals in the Highlands of Papua New Guinea and not to a ministry where we can use our musical gifts. Since God wants to refine and discipline us, we tell ourselves, naturally He will assign us to the very thing we like the least. Indeed, it is often the standing joke in many churches that when a person says he doesn't like a particular place, someone will chirp in with, "You'd better watch out. That's probably where God's going to send you." It's said jokingly, but it cuts close to the bone of what we believe to be true about the character of God. Yes, God does want to refine and discipline us, and yes, sometimes He may ask us to do things we don't enjoy doing or want to do. But more often than not, God has gifted us with natural talents and abilities because He has plans for us to use them in the furtherance of His kingdom here on earth, and to make anything else the rule is to misrepresent the character of God.

I grew up laboring under this negative spoil-sport concept of God. God was constantly on the lookout lest I did something wrong. In retrospect, it's a foolish concept, yet one I fully believed. I had no understanding then that God had created me to have fellowship with Him. Nor did I understand that fellowship with God was to be full of joy, liveliness, color, and vitality. Instead, my Christian life was a negative experience based on keeping rules. I earnestly desired to be holy, but I thought that holiness was tied to doing certain things rather than to a state of being that comes from relationship with God. Anything that was fun or exciting or smacked of too much enjoyment was obviously worldly, and if I were truly holy, God would not want me to be involved with it. Instead of finding enjoyment in life, I thought I had to be on my knees before Him in agonizing prayer. Although prayer is important and God wants us in prayer before Him, we sometimes portray prayer in such a negative way that we play it off against joy and excitement. We either pray or are enticed by the temptations of the flesh to enjoy and get excited about life. This is incorrect. Prayer is not to be cast in a negative vein as something we must do if we want to be holy. Prayer instead is a joyful and exciting experience where we come to be with the One who loves us and enjoys our company. We are holy not because of anything we do (including prayer) but because God, who is holy, has chosen us as His holy ones.

Probably hundreds, if not thousands of mid-week prayer meetings in churches across our nation have ceased to exist because people stopped attending them. We have assigned such a negative and ritualistic connotation to prayer that people no longer want to attend prayer meetings. To many Christians, prayer has become boring and largely irrelevant.

I continue to thank God that as I began to know and understand Him better I was delivered from this bondage. Suddenly prayer became alive for me. It moved from the ritualistic to the real. I was with the God who loved me, who created me for fellowship with Him, and there was no place in all the world I would rather be than in fellowship with Him through prayer. Through prayer I found real joy and excitement in life as God revealed more and more about Himself to me. I had a new freedom in my Christian life. My relationship with the Lord had moved from a negative to a positive and vibrant experience.

## Personal Application Points

1) Are preconceived ideas about God incorrect?

2) What are some of your preconceived ideas about God?

3) How have these ideas helped or hampered your relationship with God?

Chapter Five

# *MORE COMMON MISCONCEPTIONS*

*B*y now I trust you're beginning to see the devastating consequences that people's preconceived notions about God can have on their attempts to build an intimate relationship with Him. This chapter continues to examine popular misconceptions about God.

### God Is Not Too Big, Important, or Lofty to Care About His Children

As finite human beings, we often have difficulty in conceiving of God as eternal and limitless. I believe this is so because of the way we think and reason. We begin to understand things by relating and comparing them to other similar things already recorded in the experience vaults of our minds. Once such correlations have been made, we are then able to put a conceptual handle on what it is we have encountered. However, since no similar concept of eternity exists, we find it very difficult to grasp and understand the idea that God is eternal. Since we *can* conceive of the idea of duration of time, we might be able to understand an idea of God as being 100 million years old. The idea of eternity may still be hard for us to grasp, but at least we are able to put a conceptual handle on it.

The same difficulty arises when we try to conceive of God's being able to carry on an unlimited number of close, intimate relationships with people. We ask, How can God really be interested in me? How can He love me and know me and have an intimate relationship with me while He is carrying on an intimate relationship with millions of other Christians? People are able to have close and intimate relationships with only a handful of other people. They may know a large number of people on a first-name basis or as casual friends, but they can enter into intimate relationship with just a few of those people. Noticing this limitation, we carry it over to God and wonder how He could possibly intimately love and care for all the people in the world. So, we rationalize, although God is there, He is remote and cannot possibly be personally interested in each of us.

God is an unlimited being, however, and any attempt to rationalize and understand His vastness and power in the end puts limits on that vastness and power. From our finite human perspective, we will never fully understand God's vastness and power, and so we must accept that God is as the Bible declares Him to be. If the Bible tells us that God is boundless and able to love infinite numbers of people at the same time, then God is indeed able to do just that.God is not some remote, indifferent force that inhabits the cosmos. He is a loving, tender, caring, creator who cares about His creation and is intimately involved with it.

### God Is Not at All Like the God Portrayed in the Media

Much of our knowledge comes through the media, from such sources as books, radio, television, movies, newspapers, and magazines. But in many of these forms of media, God is grossly misrepresented. Most often God is projected in the media as the disinterested force behind the universe. In the news media, the fixation seems to be on the failure of people who are or claim to be Christians. This, too, is largely how Christians are depicted in the movies—ministers are portrayed as phony, bigoted, or ignorant, and Christians in general are depicted as hypocrites. Since Christians are representations of God's character, these negative portrayals paint a negative picture of the character of God.

We all like to be entertained and informed, and my purpose is not to enter into a diatribe against the media. Indeed, I like to watch the evening news on television, read books, and watch movies. My purpose here is to make us mindful of the fact that the God portrayed in the media is not the God of the Bible. More than ninety percent of those involved in all the varying forms of the media are not Christians, and we should not be hoodwinked into accepting others' concept of God. George Burns's portrayal of God may induce us to laughter, but rest assured, God is not a jovial old man who wears Ben Franklin spectacles and smokes fat cigars. That is simply a media image of God.

### God Is Not a Heavenly Projection of Ourselves

God is not a god of our own making, nor is He a projection of our personal ideals of who He should be. I struggled with this for a long time. It was hard for me to realize that God wasn't an English-speaking Caucasian. I still find it hard sometimes to think of God speaking Hindi or Greek or Chinese or Russian or French or Spanish. When thinking about God, I tend to project from my own white, middle-class American background and must keep reminding myself that God is not a white, middle-class American.

We miss totally who God is by picturing Him as a heavenly projection of ourselves. In projecting God to be like ourselves, God becomes our creation, and He becomes exactly what we want Him to be. But serving such a God can lead quickly to boredom. Since we have made God in our own image, God always likes the same things, the same people, the same situations that we like, until finally we tire of the monotony of His being exactly like us. In worshiping our God, we are not worshiping a God who is infinitely bigger and wiser than we are, who can challenge and change our lives and keep our full attention every moment of every day. We are worshiping a lesser God with whom we become easily bored.

Another trap to beware of is the way we can easily create our own image of God to justify doing the things we want to do. "God doesn't mind if I do that," we rationalize. The end result of such rationalizing is pain and despair. There are no licenses to sin in life, and sooner or later that reality will catch up with us.

God is not a lifeless projection of who we would like Him to be. To move into a relationship with Him, we must begin to see Him as He really is and not as we would like Him to be.

### God Is Not a God We Can Confine in Denominational Boxes

All misconceptions about God ultimately stem from attempts to put God into a box. But as we have already seen, God is limitless and unbounded, and attempting to put Him into a box is in essence an attempt to limit His power.

The box we most often put God into is the box of denominationalism. This is not to say that there is anything particularly wrong with belonging to a Baptist, Methodist, Presbyterian, or any other church. However, when we start making a particular church and its unique set of doctrines and rules the only way by which a person can come to know God, we have put God into a denominational box.

It is helpful if a church declares particular doctrines and beliefs so that those who believe similarly can gather together to worship God. But a statement of faith listing a church's doctrines and beliefs is just that—a statement. It's not a canonized, unchangeable document and should not be put in the place where the things listed on it become absolutes. A denomination's statement of faith and belief is not the Word of God; it is merely a subjective interpretation of His Word.

I used to be part of a church movement that put great emphasize on the fact that it had no creed but the Bible. In truth and in practice, it did have a creed, though not a uniform creed. Each church seemed to have its own creed. Each church seemed to emphasize some different aspect of scripture as it related to the nature and character of God and to daily church life. You would do something, and suddenly you were confronted by the leaders of the church over breaking the church creed. And

you would say, "I didn't think we had a creed."
"Ah, we don't," they would reply. "We move only
as the Bible tells us. We think only the thoughts
that God thinks." The problem is, of course, that
when we read the Bible to get God's thoughts, we
filter what we've read through our filters and end
up with a filtered-down version of what we have
read.

In response to questions from members of
their congregation about the meaning of a particular verse, I have heard pastors and church
leaders reply, "Well, that doesn't really mean
what it appears to say. Let me explain what it
really means." Then they roll the verse over under their doctrinal umbrella and expound on
what they think it says or what they wish it said.
We must be careful to let the Word of God say
what it says, and we are on dangerous ground
when we dismiss the plain truth of the Bible
because it doesn't align with our church's version
of the truth.

When finally we stand before God, He is not
going to ask us, "Tell me again how your pastor
understood that verse." We are all personally responsible for our own life—*our* words, actions,
beliefs, and decisions. We need to be studying the
Word of God for ourselves and believing what we
find there to be the truth. No single church has a
corner on God, and any claim by a church to be the
right one and especially the *only* right one should
immediately sound warning bells. We don't get
voted into or out of the church, and belonging to a

particular denomination does not assure us that we are a member of the true church. We become a member of the true church of Jesus Chirst by being added to it by the Father through the blood of Christ. God, and God alone—not the church—writes our name into the Book of Life. And once written there, it cannot be removed.

There are some other inherent dangers in thinking that our church has a corner on God's truth. Such thinking leads first and foremost to pride. We begin thinking we're better than the others, since we have "the truth." Out of this pride grows an isolationist mentality. Why do we need others, since we have the truth? Why don't we just keep to ourselves? There is also a tendency toward legalism as we move to institutionalize our truth. Our isolationist mentality also leads to the development of a spirit of competition where we begin to waste time and precious resources on duplication of effort because we want things done our way, since ours is the "right" way. We begin wasting our evangelistic fervor on "evangelizing" other Christians so that they will recognize and embrace the truth we so obviously have. All the while, those who have never heard the truth of the Gospel continue to go to a Christless eternity. Ultimately, we end up replacing knowing God with our church's theology and doctrine.No church has a monopoly on God's grace or good Christian character, and some Christians will be in for a surprise when they get to heaven.

Often we cling to our denominational biases

not even realizing we are biased. I never realized how many denominational biases I had until I moved from one denomination to another. I discovered then that I had many biases that I had accepted as unquestioned gospel truth and that I needed to lay aside if I was to truly embrace the new denomination.

Clinging blindly to our denominational biases and allowing them to come between us and other Christians is disobedience to the Lord. Ephesians 4:3 tells us to "Make every effort to keep the unity of the Spirit through the bond of peace." In John 17:21-23, Jesus prays that we would all be one so that through our unity the world would see Jesus and know that He is the truth. Through the unity of Christians, all people will know of God's love for them. Ephesians 4:4-5 say, "There is one body and one Spirit—just as you were called to one hope when you were called—one Lord, one faith, one baptism; one God and Father of all, who is over all and through all and in all." God works in and through all denominations; He is not limited to one denomination, and neither should we limit Him.

Denominations are like pieces of a mosaic. Up close they have different shapes and colors, and it's hard to tell how they relate to each other. But stand back a little and see how the view changes. As we see the whole, we suddenly see how the pieces relate to each other to form a beautiful design. We are often so concerned with the close-up view of our denomination that we lose sight of the broader view and fail to see how each denomination fits with the others to become a beautiful mosaic of God's truth. Different parts of that truth are embodied in the different denominations that make up the mosaic. We need each other. Each denomination and each church have a part of the truth that we need if we are to grow in our understanding of God. God will not fit into our denominational boxes, and any attempt to put Him in a box is doomed to failure.

From this and the previous chapter, we can see that the common misconceptions about God that abound today can have a great impact upon our ability to relate to God in an intimate way. Many of these misconceptions paint a picture of a God with whom we would fear intimacy or who seems to have no desire for intimacy with us. But nothing is further from the truth. God desires to have an intimate relationship with us. But for us to enter into that relationship we must let go of our broken image of God and embrace God as He truly is.

## Personal Application Points

1) As you have read these two chapters, what are some of the things you have discovered about what God is truly like?

2) How do these things compare with what you believe God to be like?

3) What are some practical ways you might integrate into your daily life any new discoveries you have made about what God is like?

## Chapter Six

# *GOD, OUR FATHER*

*H*aving discussed what God is not, we now turn our attention to discovering who God is and how we can develop a deep and intimate relationship with Him. Just what *is* God like? Jesus, who in human form was the exact image of God, provides us with the answer. All that Jesus is, God is—kind, loving, concerned, patient, understanding, just, caring, righteous, and perfect. I suspect that most of us already know that God has all those attributes. We can see the various elements of God embodied in the misconceptions we looked at in the two previous chapters. But more than knowing what God is like, our key to an intimate relationship with Him is knowing how to relate to Him. We know that God embodies all these wonderful qualities, but how do we relate to such a being? How should we approach Him? What do we call Him?

Jesus again provides the answer. He related to God as His Father. He also pointed out to His disciples that God was to be their Father. When you pray to God, Jesus told His disciples, "you should pray: 'Our Father in heaven' " (Matthew 6:9). Since God is our Father, we are to relate to Him as our Father.

## Old Testament Revelation of God as our Father

The importance and place of a father is central to the Old Testament. Old Testament Jewish society was patriarchal, which is reflected in the number of references to father in the Old Testament. In the book of Genesis alone, there are 195 references to father or fathers. The importance of the father is enhanced in Exodus 20:12 when Moses tells the people to "Honor your father and mother, so that you may live long in the land the Lord your God is giving you." This, of course, is one of the Ten Commandments that the Lord delivered to Moses on Mount Sinai, and it shows the importance God places upon fathers (and mothers).

Respect for a father is important in the Old Testament. "Each of you must respect his mother and father...I am the Lord your God" (Leviticus

19:3). The gravity of failing to respect one's father is illustrated in the next chapter of Leviticus: "If anyone curses his father or mother, he must be put to death. He has cursed his father or his mother, and his blood will be on his own head" (Leviticus 20:9). The theme of respecting your father and the consequences of not doing so is played out again and again throughout the history of the Jews as recorded in the Old Testament.

Despite this emphasis on honoring and respecting our earthly father, the Old Testament has little to say about loving our father, although the idea of love is implicit in the command to respect our father. Nonetheless, the Old Testament presents none of the warm, loving father-child relationship that is revealed in the New Testament and held up as a model for us as to how we should relate to God.

David is really the first of the Old Testament writers to introduce the idea of God as our Father. It was David who introduced the idea of God as the father of Israel. Previously God had always been referred to as the "God of our father Abraham" or the "God of our forefathers." In 1 Chronicles 29:10, though, David blesses the Lord saying, "Blessed *be* thou, LORD God of Israel our father, for ever and ever"(KJV). David also likens God to a father in the Psalms: "A father to the fatherless, a defender of widows, is God in his holy dwelling" (Psalm 68:5) and "As a father has compassion on his children, so the LORD has compassion on those who fear him" (Psalm 103:13). Solomon also picks up this theme in Proverbs 3:11-12 when he says, "My son, do not despise the LORD's discipline and do not resent his rebuke, because the LORD disciplines those he loves, as a father the son he delights in."

The prophet Isaiah also refers to God as Father: "But you are our Father,...you, O LORD, are our Father, our Redeemer from of old is your name" (Isaiah 63:16) and "Yet, O LORD, you are our Father. We are the clay, you are the potter; we are all the work of your hand" (Isaiah 64:8).

The great revelation of God as a father in the Old Testament, however, comes from God Himself. Speaking through the prophet Jeremiah, God says, "I myself said, 'How gladly would I treat you like sons and give you a desirable land, the most beautiful inheritance of any nation.' I thought you would call me 'Father' and not turn away from following me. But like a woman unfaithful to her husband, so you have been unfaithful to me, O house of Israel," (Jeremiah 3:19). And through Malachi, God declares, "'A son honors his father, and a servant his master. If I am a father, where is the honor due me? If I am a master, where is the respect due me?' says the LORD Almighty" (Malachi 1:6).

These verses reveal a great deal about the relationship God wants to have with His people. God wants to be a father, to reach out with love and compassion to His sons and daughters and bear them up in times of adversity. In return, He wants His people to respond to Him with the same love and respect they have for their earthly fathers.

These verses also reveal the hurt God feels when He is rejected by His people. It is the same hurt a human father feels when his son or daughter rejects him. We sense in these verses the agony God feels when, despite all His best efforts, His people reject Him and turn away from Him.

The fuller revelation, though, of God as our Father occurs in the New Testament, particularly in the gospels. Jesus was God incarnate. His character was the focused reflection of the character of God the Father. Through studying His life, we begin to understand more fully the idea that God is indeed our Father.

## New Testament Revelation of God as Our Father

During Jesus' time, many people had difficulty understanding the way Jesus related to God as His heavenly Father. Worship of God was very formalized and centered on the synagogue and the performance of certain rituals. To have someone come along and speak about God in the familiar and intimate way that a human father and son would talk was quite a departure from what people were used to. By speaking in such a way, Jesus was laying the foundation for knowing God in a new way—as our Father.

Not only did Jesus speak about His Father in heaven, but He also provided Himself as a living example of how His followers could live out such a relationship in their everyday lives. Step by step,

He modeled for His disciples the way they could also relate to God as their father.

Jesus spoke often about our Father in heaven and how we are His sons and daughters. The following verses from the Sermon on the Mount illustrate well how Jesus viewed God as our Father:

> *"Blessed are the peacemakers, for they will be called sons of God."* (Matthew 5:9)

> *"[L]et your light shine before men, that they may see your good deeds and praise your Father in heaven."* (Matthew 5:16)

> *"But I tell you: Love your enemies and pray for those who persecute you, that you may be sons of your Father in heaven."* (Matthew 5:44-45)

> *"Be perfect, therefore, as your heavenly Father is perfect."* (Matthew 5:48)

> *"But love your enemies....Then your reward will be great, and you will be sons of the Most High, because he is kind to the ungrateful and wicked. Be merciful, just as your Father is merciful."* (Luke 6:35-36)

> *"Be careful not to do your 'acts of righteousness' before men, to be seen by them. If you do, you will have no reward from your Father in heaven."* (Matthew 6:1)

> *"But when you give to the needy, do not let your left hand know what your right hand is doing, so that your giving may be in secret. Then your Father, who sees what is done in secret, will reward you."* (Matthew 6:3-4)

> *"But when you pray, go into your room, close the door and pray to your Father, who is unseen. Then your Father, who sees what is done in secret, will reward you."* (Matthew 6:6)

> *"...your Father knows what you need before you ask him. This, then, is how you should pray: Our Father in heaven, hallowed be your name,..."* (Matthew 6:8-9)

In these verses, Jesus shifts the focus from God as His Father to God as *our* Father.

Many people have confessed to me that they find it easy to relate to Jesus but encounter great difficulty in relating to God as a father. They think Jesus is much more accessible, understanding, and forgiving than God the Father. But this is not so, since Jesus and the Father are one. Jesus said, "Anyone who has seen me has seen the Father" (John 14:9). Since Jesus is the focused reflection of the character of God the Father, all that Jesus is, the Father is. Jesus is not more forgiving or understanding than the Father. Yes, Jesus is understanding, approachable, and forgiving, and so is the Father. God the Father is not a stern, surly old man in the sky. He and Jesus are the same. To know the one's character is to know the other's. Jesus came into this world as part of God's plan to reconcile us to Himself and to bring fresh revelation and understanding of God's character—that God is a father who loves His children.

So God is our Father. But what kind of father is He? We'll explore this question in the next chapter.

## Personal Application Points

1) Have you ever before considered that God wants you to relate to Him as your Father?

2) Has your relationship with the Lord been more centered around Jesus or around knowing God as your Father?

3) What are some steps you can take to embrace God as your Father in your life?

Chapter Seven

# *GOD'S CHARACTER AS A FATHER*

*I*f God is our Father, the obvious questions that present themselves are, How is God a Father to us? What is His character as a Father? What can we expect of him as our Father? What sort of father is He to His children? This chapter looks closely at these questions and discusses a number of aspects of God as our Father.

**God Is Our Creator**

Without God we would not exist. God created

and fashioned us after His own image and nature. He made us the people we are and breathed into us His breath. "For in him we live and move and have our being....'We are his offspring' "(Acts 17:28). "So God created man in his own image, in the image of God he created him; male and female he created them" (Genesis 1:27).

## God Is Our Protector

In love God guards, defends, and shields His children from harm. "How priceless is your unfailing love! Both high and low among men find refuge in the shadow of your wings" (Psalm 36:7). Jesus captures this protective nature of God in the parable of the shepherd who leaves his ninety-nine other sheep to go and search for one lost sheep that has strayed from the flock. "In the same way your Father in heaven is not willing that any of these little ones should be lost" (Matthew 18:14).

Each of us is like this one lost sheep, and God will not let us go. When we lose our way in life, or when danger is near, God will search for us and surround us with His protection. He is the one who firmly holds our hand and guides us, and He will not let go of our hand. If we do lose our way and fall into sin, it's not because God has let go of our hand but because we, through yielding to temptation or through will-full disobedience, have removed our hand from His grip. "[N]o one can snatch them out of my Father's hand" (John 10:29).

## God Is Our Provider

"So do not worry, saying, 'What shall we eat?'...your heavenly Father knows what you need" (Matthew 6:31-32). "And my God will meet all your needs according to his glorious riches in Christ Jesus" (Philippians 4:19). God anticipates and meets the needs of His children. (Note, however, that while He supplies all the needs of His children, He does not necessarily provide all their wants.)

## God Is Our Instructor

"Listen, my sons, to a father's instruction; pay attention and gain understanding [insight]" (Proverbs 4:1). "I will instruct you and teach you in the way you should go; I will counsel you and watch over you" (Psalm 32:8). Note that God's instruction is designed to give us insight into how God wants us to live, insight we can apply to all our situations in life. Such insight comes through a number of means: through daily reading and meditating upon God's Word, through prayer, through anointed and appointed spiritual leadership, and through worship.

## God Is Our Corrector

Following from instruction comes correction. Like any loving parent, God takes the time to correct and discipline His children. Yet often He is misunderstood in this. God is not vindictive. He does not punish or bring correction to His children because He enjoys doing so. He does it because He loves them. A loving father teaches his child about the dangers of fire and scolds him when he uses matches carelessly. He scolds the child because he loves him. The child may not be aware of the danger that careless playing with matches can cause and thus may feel that his being scolded is unjustified. However, as time passes, the child grows in his understanding of the danger of playing with matches and sees the loving intent of his father and the justice of being corrected.

So too with God. He has our best interests at heart. From our limited understanding, there will be times when we wonder about God's motivation in correcting us, especially when the correction is an unpleasant experience. However, as time passes and we begin to understand more about God and how He wants us to live our lives, we come to see His loving intent toward us. He corrects us because He loves us, and for no other reason: "My son, do not despise the LORD's discipline and do not resent his rebuke, because the LORD disciplines those he loves, as a father the son he delights in" (Proverbs 3:11-12).

"Yet, O LORD, you are our Father. We are the clay, you are the potter; we are all the work of your hand" (Isaiah 64:8). God wants to shape and mold us into the people He wants us to be, and part of that process includes trials and hardships.

## God Is Our Redeemer

"[A]s far as the east is from the west, so far has he removed our transgressions from us. As a father has compassion on his children, so the LORD has compassion on those who fear him" (Psalm 103:12-13). God forgives our faults and failures and redeems our lives.

Perhaps the best portrait of God and His forgiveness at work is found in the parable of the prodigal son (Luke 15:11-32). In the parable, a father, despite his grieving heart and knowledge of the outcome of his son's actions, respects his son's decision to leave home. The father doesn't go after his son seeking to rescue him. Instead, he waits patiently for the consequences of the son's leaving to take their toll. He allows his son to reap the harvest of his own rebellion. However, when the son, having suffered the consequences of his rebellion, comes to his senses and decides to return home, the father greets his son with joy and celebration. The parable teaches us much about how God responds to us, his children. When we turn our back on Him, His heart is full of sorrow and grief, yet when we return to Him, He is full of joy. While God will let us go when we choose to deliberately walk away from Him, Christ's atoning death shows us the lengths to which our heavenly Father will go to draw us back to Him.

## God Is Our Comforter

"Praise be to the God and Father of our Lord Jesus Christ, the Father of compassion and the God of all comfort, who comforts us in all our troubles, so that we can comfort those in any trouble with the comfort we ourselves have received from God" (2 Corinthians 1:3-4). God comforts us. He loves us and cares about us. In times of distress, grief, or pain He does not leave us alone but draws near to us. He weeps with us. He understands how we feel. He hurts with us. We know we are not alone, that someone is there with us who understands what we are feeling and is helping us to bear our sorrows, our hurts, and our disappointments.

The one thread that runs through all of these things that God is to us as our Father is love. God is a God of love, and God's love is demonstrated in every aspect of His character. Love is the key to a relationship with God as our Father. We see the love He has for us, and we are drawn to respond to Him in love. "We love because he first loved us" (1 John 4:19).

This love, however, is not the greeting card sentimentality often associated with love today. God's love is derived from and driven by His desire for our greatest good. God created us and knows us better than we know ourselves. As a result, He knows what is best for our lives. He knows what our greatest good is, who it is He created us to be, and what it is He wants us to do with our lives. Such knowledge motivates God's actions as He seeks to lead us to our greatest good. Thus, God's love is a very practical love, motivated by a desire to see us become all that He created us to be.

In John 14:8-10, Philip is having difficulty understanding the Father, so Jesus spells things out for him: "Anyone who has seen me has seen the Father" (John 14:19). As we study the life of Jesus, we are in fact studying the nature and character of God the Father. Jesus reflects the character of the Father in thought (John 8:55), word (John 8:28), deed (John 5:19, 6:18), and name (John 10:25). Thus, we must lay aside any doubts we may have about the character of God the Father. God is love, and the character of Jesus flows straight from the character of His Father.

## Personal Application Points

1) Pick one of the areas discussed and share an experience from your life of how God revealed Himself to you in that way.

2) Are there some areas where you need to experience God in that way? What are they?

3) List some practical steps you could take to experience God in that way.

Chapter Eight

# *THE QUESTION OF*
# *SUFFERING*

*A*ny discussion about God being our Father must address the inevitable question that arises: If God is my Heavenly Father and truly loves me, why does He let me suffer? This is a reasonable question to ask, since all of us at some time in our lives suffer disappointments and discomforts. Why do they happen? Why does God allow them?

In answering such questions, we must first put things in perspective. As human beings we tend to look only at the negative side of life. But we must remember that there is also a positive side. There are times when God has protected and delivered us from our circumstances: the accident we were involved in when we should have been killed but miraculously were not, the time when God removed a person from the scene who was causing us much pain and suffering, the time when deep within we discovered a reservoir of strength that allowed us to face and conquer a situation rather than walk away from it or be hurt by it. These are times when God has intervened on our behalf to deliver or protect us from situations that had the potential to cause us both physical and emotional pain and suffering. We all have such testimonies, not to mention the times when God stepped in on our behalf when we weren't even aware of it!

The first thing to note is that God does protect and deliver us from situations that have the potential to cause suffering. Yet hurt and disappointment do befall us as Christians. I have experienced great suffering in my own life in recent years. The first was the death of my wife Betty after a seven-year battle with cancer. Her death was very difficult and devastating for me to endure. Three years later, my oldest son Mark died of melanoma cancer. He was thirty-seven years old and left a wife and four children under the age of seven. I struggled for answers. My confidence in God's faithfulness was deeply shaken. Why had He allowed such suffering to happen? Was His character not really as consistent as the Bible declares it to be? I struggled for answers.

I found my answer in Isaiah 55:8-9: "'For my thoughts are not your thoughts, neither are your ways my ways,' declares the LORD. 'As the heavens are higher than the earth, so are my ways higher than your ways and my thoughts than your thoughts.'" I had to accept by faith that in all that had happened, God had good in it for me and for all those in my family who had suffered as a result of Betty's and Mark's deaths. I didn't fully understand what that good was, but I accepted it as part of God's plan for my life. God's intentions are infinite, and while I cannot fully understand those intentions, my lack of understanding in no way diminishes them. Indeed, God has brought many changes to my life as a result of the loss of my wife and my son. With a personal knowledge of what it is like to suffer the loss of a loved one, I have more empathy and compassion for those similarly suffering. I have gained new insights into the nature and character of God. And God has provided me with a wonderful new wife in answer to my prayers. All of these things have helped to restore my confidence in God's character.

God is not the author of the suffering and tragedies that befall our world. Man is. God gave man a free will, and in the exercise of that free will, man has chosen to upset the divine balance through willful disobedience to God's established laws. Death is a result of man's wrong choices. It is part of the curse God placed upon Adam and Eve for disobedience to His direct command not to eat from the tree of the knowledge of good and evil. Since that time, death has come to each person who has ever lived.

As we look around our world today, we continually see evidence of suffering that is the result of man's sinful choices. In Somalia and Ethiopia, for example, people are starving to death by the tens of thousands. In the midst of two bloody civil wars in this famine-stricken region, evil and repressive governments and rebel factions alike are stopping the flow of food and relief aid to the innocent people who so desperately need it. Each side believes that its action will bring the opposing faction to its knees in surrender. But surrender hasn't taken place—only pain and suffering for hundreds of thousands of innocent and starving people.

Horrors are also occurring in Yugoslavia. The suffering, pain, and hardships of that country are the result of deeply rooted bitterness in the hearts of men who mistakenly believe that the only way to resolve differences is to fight to the end, regardless of the cost in human suffering. There are the tragedies of Northern Ireland, of South Africa, of India, and of so many other places around the world where there is human pain and suffering. And in all of these places, the suffering is a direct result of man's inhumanity against his fellow man which, in turn, is a result of man's choice to turn his back on God and take matters into his own hands, choosing to hate his fellow man instead of loving him as God commands.

What about those of us who live in the Western world? Where does the suffering we experience come from? The answer is the same—from other people. Our suffering may have arisen through out-of-control relationships within our family. It may have arisen from a business deal in which we were swindled out of money we work-ed hard to earn. It may have arisen from some other criminal activity fostered upon us. Whatever the cause, our suffering is a direct result of the selfish decisions of people. The final truth is that man, through disobedience and wrong choices, is the author and originator of much suffering.

What can God do in light of all this suffering? Scripture declares that God's heart is broken and grieved by the suffering He sees in the world, especially when it is the result of deliberate choices on the part of man. "I have been grieved by their adulterous hearts, which have turned away from me, and by their eyes, which have lusted after their idols" (Ezekiel 6:9). Yet despite his grief, God will not violate man's free will. God created man in His image, which ultimately entails a degree of personal sovereignty and freedom to choose. With that sovereignty, man can choose to love God or reject Him, and God will not interfere with man's choices. God wants us to love Him because we choose to love Him for who He is and not because, like some automaton, we are unable to make any other choice.

God never stops loving those who reject Him. God's love expresses itself as grief as God is forced to release a person to the folly of his or her choice in the hope that ultimately the person will come to his or her senses and accept Him.

Indeed, His love for mankind has led God to suffer the greatest of all grief—that of seeing His own Son suffer and die for the redemption of mankind. Yet despite this greatest of all sacrifices, pain and suffering continue unabated because people continue to rebel against God. And the world will continue to suffer the consequences of man's rebellion until Christ's return.

Thus we are all—Christian and non-Christian— victims of the suffering of an imperfect world whose imperfection is the result of our own and others' rebellion against God. We are not abandoned, though, to this suffering without any hope. We began this chapter by observing that God does intervene on our behalf to shield and protect us from situations that have the potential to cause us pain and suffering. When God does not step in to shield and protect us, we have the promise of Romans 8:28 to cling to: "And we know that in all things God works for the good of those who love him, who have been called according to his purpose."

When my three children were growing up, they each faced a variety of situations and challenges, some of which had the potential to cause great pain and suffering. There were times when, as their father, I would step in and rescue them from a potentially hurtful situation. Yet there were other times when I stood back and let them deal with a situation on their own. This was not always easy to do. It pains parents greatly to watch their child suffer. And when parents do not rush into a situation to rescue their child, it does not mean they do not love the child. Rather, the opposite is true. I sometimes let my children face situations on their own *because* I loved them and because I knew that the lessons they would learn through facing a situation and the ensuing character growth they would experience would far outweigh my urge to shield them. I am sure my children didn't always understand why I didn't always bail them out. But I had a plan, and now that they are grown, the results of that plan are clearly evident in their strength of character.

God deals with us in much the same way. His desire is to perfect us as Christians. Because God wants our character to be strong and deeply-rooted, He uses our daily situations towards this end. He is not out to hurt us, and He will step in if a situation becomes more than we can handle. He never asks us to bear our burdens alone. His intentions are always loving and focused on our greatest good and on seeing that good brought to fruition.

We are not immune to the tragedies and hurts that cause suffering in life. There are times when God shields us from them, and there are times when He does not. What is important about suffering is our attitude towards it, because our attitude will determine whether or not the situation will strengthen our character. If we face situations with a negative attitude, we will see only pain and suffering and will soon have a negative outlook on life that ultimately leads to bitterness and despair at God and others over our predicament. However, if our attitude is positive, we see that God has our greatest good at heart. We see that He is using a situation to help us develop strength of character so that we can be made more like Jesus. When we begin to see things this way, we will embrace every situation, no matter how difficult the situation may seem at the time, because we know it is part of God's eternal plan and purpose for our life. Suffering can be a very positive and powerful force as we are molded to be more like Jesus. Suffering causes us to rely on God even more than we did before, and as we do this, we begin to understand more of His ways and the love He has for us.

Suffering also causes us to be dependent upon God and upon other Christians. In our individualistic society, it is easy to cut ourselves off from others. But this is not God's purpose for us. We are to be dependent upon Him and upon one another in love. Suffering draws us to others as they seek to love and comfort us through the difficulties we face. And of course, as this happens, our life becomes a message to those around us of God's love and faithfulness. Our suffering also builds a sense of compassion into our heart for others who may also be suffering.

All that we must do to reap the benefits of suffering in our lives is to open ourselves up and embrace it, trusting as we do so that God is working His eternal plan and purpose into us.

## Personal Application Points

1) Have you had difficulty in the past understanding how God could allow suffering?

2) Do the points presented in this chapter help you answer your questions about suffering?

3) Will the insights of this chapter change the way you look at and handle suffering in the future?

Chapter Nine

# *HINDRANCES TO KNOWING GOD AS OUR FATHER*

*I*n any discussion of God as our Father, we need to ask several questions: What does the word *father* mean to you? What kind of images does the word evoke for you? Does it call up a picture of a warm, loving, caring person? Or does it perhaps bring to mind a stern, distant figure or an angry, unreasonable man? A different image of Father springs to mind for each of us. Our concept of a father is determined by our relationship with our own father. If our father was harsh and unreasonable, most likely our concept of a father will be of a harsh and unreasonable person. If, on the other hand, our father was loving and kind, we would tend to think of a father along those lines. If we grew up without a father or if our father was emotionally unavailable, we may think of a father as someone who is unapproachable. Thus, past experience defines for us the mental images we associate with the word *father*.

What we think of when we hear the word *father* has an obvious bearing on how we relate to God. If our concept of a father is colored by negative experiences from our past, chances are we will experience difficulty in relating to God as our Father. We will carry over onto God an erroneous understanding of His character based upon the inadequacies of our relationship with our father. Yet to enter into the full relationship that God desires to have with us, it is important that we come to know Him as our Father.

We spoke in the previous chapters about understanding God's character as a father, but this is very different from experiencing God as our Father. As previously pointed out, a loving relationship is not based on knowledge about a person but is based on intimate experience with the person. We love the other person, who experiences our love for him or her, and in turn we experience the love he or she has for us.

So it is with God our Father. He wants us to experience the love He has for us, and in turn He wants to experience the love we have for Him. For many of us, this is where the difficulty begins. We find it hard to both give and receive love from others. Often the root of this problem lies in our experiences as children in relating to our parents, family, and friends.

This chapter looks at some of the difficulties we face in relating to God as our Father and the reason for these difficulties. Armed with a new understanding, we will then be able to deal with our problems and move into truly experiencing God as our Father.

Although many of the difficulties we face in relating to God as our Father arise because of problems we had in our relationship with our parents, this does not necessarily mean that our parents intentionally made our relationship with them awkward or hard. Parents are fallible. They make mistakes. George's experience illustrates this point well.

George grew up in Japan, where his parents were missionaries. He was a normal boy, inquisitive and happy. But his parents were very busy with their work, and when George asked his father questions, his father would gruffly say, "George, grow up! I'm too busy for this nonsense." One day George decided to take his father's advice. He figured it was time to stop being a little boy, and he became a little man. His busy parents were very pleased with his move to premature adulthood. Years later, though, after George had married and was raising his own family, he found he couldn't relate to his children. He had no empathy or compassion for them, which created major communication problems with his children as well as with his wife. Finally George sought help from a professional counselor. Through counseling he was able to get to the root of his problem. He had never had an adolescence. In being too busy trying to be an adult, he had never allowed himself to be a teenager. Through counseling he was able to deal with and overcome his problem and restore his relationship with his wife and children.

George's parents hadn't set out to create this situation for George. I'm sure that had they foreseen the results, they would not have continued to tell George to grow up. But they believed, given their circumstances, that they were doing the best for their son. They were not deliberately being malicious; rather, they were just trying to be good parents. But their best efforts inadvertently caused a great problem for George that he had to overcome later in life.

If we have encountered a similar situation in our life, there is only one solution—forgive our parents. Most likely our parents were not even aware of the consequences of what they were doing. While most parents desire the best for their children, occasionally their choice of what is best can lead to hurt in a child. This hurt is often locked away inside and doesn't surface until some later event nudges it free.

There are other things that some of us have

experienced that adversely affect our ability to relate to God as a father.

## Fatherless Children

Some may have lost their father as a child through death, divorce, or abandonment. Such an experience leads to feelings of loss, emptiness, and desertion. These people grow up with no model of a father. As a result, it becomes difficult for them to relate to someone wanting to fill that position at a later time in their life.

Dan and Julie are brother and sister. Their father died when they were twelve and fourteen, respectively. Without their father to guide and love them, they began to lose direction. They both became involved in drugs. They dropped out of church, and their lives began to fall apart. As adults, Dan and Julie both married, but their marriages didn't last. Messy divorces wreaked more havoc in their lives. Indeed, it has been very difficult for them to maintain any kind of stability in their lives. The hurts and wounds that have come from being left fatherless have marked their lives deeply and hindered their attempts to relate to God as their heavenly Father.

## Embittered Children

Some people have experienced fathers who had little time for them when they were children. Sometimes this was because of the father's misplaced priorities. Perhaps the father thought that the best way to be a father to his children was to work hard and provide all his children's physical wants and needs. Unfortunately, in doing so he overlooked the most important need of his children—love and togetherness. Or perhaps because of selfishness, the father refused to take responsibility for his children and instead let them go their own way without giving the love or direction they desperately needed. As a result, the children grow up feeling embittered towards their father. They become angry with their father, and many girls subsequently become angry at men in general. Later in life, angry and bitter feelings are easily carried over into how such people think about and relate to God.

I remember a young man who came to the Salem, Oregon, Youth With a Mission center to attend a discipleship training school. The man was so bitter over the hurts created by his parents' divorce that he was unable to function normally. As a result of his hurt and bitterness and out of a deep need to find love and acceptance, he had become involved in adultery. He began living with a woman who already had a child out of wedlock. The relationship eventually broke up, creating further pain and bitterness for this young man. The man began getting into trouble, first with the police and then with his employer. A pattern of defeat followed by loss of confidence developed in his life. To avoid the pain this cycle invariably brought, the man turned to drugs. Soon his life was in ruins. The feelings of rejection and bitterness he had encountered as a result of his parents' divorce had led him down a destructive path of wrong choices.

Finally this young man became a Christian, but he experienced great difficulty in relating to God as a father. While in Salem we shared and prayed with him, and changes began to take place in his life. Soon it was hard to recognize him as the same person. He seemed well on the road to recovery and wholeness. Unfortunately, when he returned home, he began focusing again on the hurt and bitterness in his life. All he began to talk about was how badly he had been treated by his parents. Soon he was right back in the old cycle, living with another woman and back on drugs. Over the years he has taken steps to try to get his life back in order. He desires to serve God, but he faces a long and difficult road to wholeness. Yet he is like so many others today who are trapped in a web of bitterness because of hurts they received from their parents while growing up.

## Ignored Children

Some people have never felt loved and appreciated by their father. Victorian ethics and the macho man myth have made it very difficult for some men to express their true feelings, especially feelings of love for others. Many have learned this pattern of behavior from their parents and as a result find it difficult to hold their own children and show love and affection. This does not necessarily mean they don't love their children, only that they find it hard to physically express their feelings. Children, though, need and expect the physical affection of their father. When it is not forthcoming, they begin to feel ignored and alone.

Children can also feel ignored when their father is overly permissive. Children need and want boundaries to be set for them. Such boundaries show that parents are concerned about their children. When a father fails to set these boundaries or when the boundaries are so loose as to be pointless, the child feels ignored. When a child announces to his father that he is going out and is not sure when he will be home and the father says, "Okay, that's fine. Come home when you feel like it," the child feels a lack of love and concern. "My father doesn't even care when I'll be home," the child tells himself.

Feeling ignored and alone in turn leads to feelings of worthlessness and inferiority. With these feelings often comes an urge, almost a compulsion, to excel at something and be noticed by others to cover the inadequacies felt as a result of the relationship with one's father.

I felt ignored by my father as I was growing up. I was the tenth child in our family, and my father never once came to watch me in a game of high school football or basketball. Now, I wasn't an athletic superstar, but nevertheless, it always hurt me that he never came to watch me play. As a result, I developed a tremendous need to excel at something and be noticed so that I could prove to my father I was good enough. Much of my early life was filled with a competitive spirit as I tried to win my father's approval.

Recently a business associate shared with me that he was on his third marriage. Most of his life, he explained, had been centered on trying to prove himself to others by gaining material possessions. All his life he had never felt loved or accepted, but he knew he could excel at making money. He could prove his value to other people by making money. Unfortunately, it had not been that easy. His first two marriages had ended in shambles, and his children had lost their respect for him. Inside him was a voice that drove him on in the pursuit of possessions. Everything he had, he told me, he would willingly give up just to break his compulsion to try to prove himself through excelling.

This desire to excel creates difficulties in relating to God, because God is not interested in how well we do something. He is interested only in who we are. He loves us for who we are, and it is very hard for some people to accept love that they feel they haven't earned. But we can't earn love, since love is a gift.

## Unwanted Children

When I was about four or five years old, my mom took me with her to a quilting bee, where I crawled around and played under the quilt the women were making. As I was playing away enjoying myself, I heard my mother tell the other women that she hadn't really wanted me. She told them that when she was forty years old she didn't think she could get pregnant, but she did get pregnant with me. I listened as she explained what a disappointment it had been to discover she was pregnant again. I was stunned and hurt. Of course, when I reached age forty myself, I understood my mother's reluctance to have her tenth child. Nonetheless, at the time of the incident, it caused me great emotional pain.

Perhaps you have experienced a similar situation. Perhaps your father wanted a boy and instead got a girl, or vice versa, and he let you know that you were not really what he wanted. Perhaps your birth was an accident and your father let you know from the start that you were not planned. Such experiences can lead to feelings of being unwanted. In turn, you find it hard to accept that God wants you just as you are, that He made you, and that regardless of what your parents may think, you were planned by God to be the person you are.

Several young people have stayed with us over the years. One of them was a young woman who struggled during her growing-up years because she felt unwanted. The confusion of moving back and forth between her divorced parents and never feeling like she fit in caused her to seek love in inappropriate ways. But as she experienced healing of these earlier hurts and began to know God as her loving and faithful heavenly Father, her relationship with her earthly father was restored. It was truly amazing to see the changes that took place in her life. The woman gained a new confidence in God and a confidence in herself as she came to realize that God wanted her, designed her, and made her to be the person she was.

## Threatened Children

. Perhaps you were threatened as a child. Perhaps you had a very authoritarian father who, instead of using love and trust, used threats and bribes to discipline you. Perhaps God was sometimes used as a threat: "You do that one more time, and you know what God will do to you." Such threats can result in the feeling that God could not possibly forgive anything you have done, and that you have committed unpardonable sins. Thus, you don't know how to be close to God or relate to Him.

## Abused and Battered Children

Child abuse has reached epidemic proportions in the United States and embraces a wide gamut of forms from sexual to physical to verbal to emotional abuse. Child abuse almost always leads to deep emotional wounds and scars aside from any obvious physical ones. It can lead to hatred and resentment of the person who caused the abuse, often a father, a stepfather, or or other father figures, such as a mother's boyfriend. Abuse also produces helplessness and a broken spirit. Father becomes a dirty word, and relating to God as our heavenly Father becomes almost impossible. The thought of such a relationship creates inner turmoil and conflict.

## Dominated Children

When a dictatorial father tries to dominate his child's life, such domination leads to inner resentment and frustration within the child that often manifest as external rebellion. It is difficult for a person who has spent his or her life rebelling against a dominating father to understand why he or she should submit to God as heavenly Father.

## Pampered Children

A pampered child is one who had a pushover dad who continually gave in and gave the child anything he or she wanted. Pampered children quickly lose respect for their father. They love their father only according to how he supplies their demands. People who have been pampered as children carry this attitude into their relationship with God. They expect God to pamper them, and they continually make demands upon Him. They see Him as their errand boy in the sky. God becomes the supplier of all their desires. However, God's refusal to act as an errand boy and provide their every whim usually causes their faith to falter.

Not long ago I listened to the testimony of a young woman who shared how she'd been pampered by her father and given everything she wanted except the thing she needed the most—his love. She became a Christian and felt that she could have anything she wanted and that God would let her do whatever she pleased. She decided to experiment with drugs and soon became hooked. When she finally began to deal with her drug problem, she started to receive the discipline she badly needed. She came to realize that God was much greater and more worthy to be worshiped than she had realized and that His commandments were indeed good and she stopped treating them as the "Ten Suggestions."

## Unloved Children

Growing up feeling unloved is devastating. Such a feeling often arises when a father is unable to express his true feelings of love towards his children. Unloved children often begin looking for substitutes for the love they are lacking from a parent. For many, this leads to immorality, which in turn leads to condemnation and guilt. Riddled with guilt about past actions, such people have great difficulty asking for God's forgiveness and accepting His love.

The preceding are some of the hindrances to our seeking to know and experience God as our Father. For those caught in their grip, any of these hindrances seem insurmountable. But they are not. There is no situation we face that God cannot help us to deal with. God's desire is for us to be free from the encumbrances of the past. He wants to help us, and the next chapter shows us how we can allow Him to help us. Understanding the roots of the problem is the first step. Allowing God to deal with them is the next.

## Personal Application Points

1) What was your father like? What were his strengths and weaknesses?

2) List three positive or negative childhood experiences that helped you to form your concept of Father.

3) Can you identify any areas in your life that as a result of negative childhood experiences hold you back in relating to God as your Father?

Chapter Ten

# *FINDING FREEDOM*

*T*he good news is that those of us who have experienced any of the situations presented in the previous chapter no longer need to live under their shadow. We can find find freedom from the experiences of the past that still hold us in bondage. This chapter will help us to find this freedom.

Every problem laid out in Chapter 9 exists within one or more of the following four component areas: sin, the flesh, past hurts, and bondages. Jesus, in His various roles as Redeemer, Sanctifier, Healer, and Deliverer, is the only one who can help us to deal with these problems. The diagram in figure 3 shows how this works:

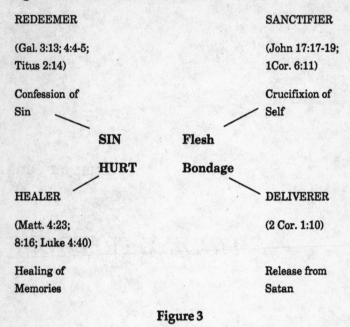

REDEEMER                              SANCTIFIER

(Gal. 3:13; 4:4-5;                    (John 17:17-19;
Titus 2:14)                           1Cor. 6:11)

Confession of                         Crucifixion of
Sin                                   Self

        **SIN**        **Flesh**

        **HURT**       **Bondage**

HEALER                                DELIVERER

(Matt. 4:23;                          (2 Cor. 1:10)
8:16; Luke 4:40)

Healing of                            Release from
Memories                              Satan

**Figure 3**

How does the process work? If the problem we are dealing with falls within the area of sin, we first need to repent and confess the sin. We then need to allow Jesus as Redeemer to forgive the sin and cleanse us from its stain upon our life.

If the problem is with the flesh, we need Jesus as Sanctifier to come and work in our life. When we know that the root of the problem is the flesh, that is where the problem needs to be dealt with. We need to crucify the problem, incident, or habit and allow Jesus to sanctify our flesh.

If we are hurting, we need healing. We need to

allow Jesus as restore us to health and to emotional wholeness to our lives.

If we are in bondage to something, we need to be delivered from it and experience Jesus as our Deliverer.

This simple chart has been very helpful to me, both in dealing with problem areas in my own life and in counseling others. When I'm counseling someone who says, "I have this problem in my life," I respond, "Tell me about the problem." As the person relates the problem, I question the person and try to discover into which area the primary cause of the problem falls. When I know the source of the problem, I can then deal effectively with the problem.

In medicine, since there is no single drug that cures all illnesses, it would be absurd for a doctor to prescribe one medicine for all ailments. Instead, a doctor makes a diagnosis by ascertaining what the problem is and then applies the right cure. So too in the spiritual realm. There is no single cure for all that ails us spiritually. First we must ascertain what the problem is so we can apply the right cure. If a person's problem is in the area of sin, casting it out is the wrong medicine. The proper cure for sin is confession and repentance so that we can receive forgiveness.

This may seem academic, but as I've counseled with people over the years I have been astounded at how many never receive the freedom and victory they seek. Most often this is because they do not seek the right cure. They do not deal with the problem in the way it should be dealt with. So they struggle on with the problem, often feeling defeated and dejected.

If we are to experience victory over problem areas in our lives, then we must use the right medicine. Let me illustrate this point further. My oldest son Mark developed severe pain in and around his ear. He went to the doctor, who looked in his ear with his light and then prescribed some eardrops. But the drops didn't work, and the pain persisted. Finally, Mark sought the opinion of another doctor, who looked further than the immediate symptoms of an earache. The doctor wanted to get to the root of the problem and ran some tests and found that the source of the earache was a severe recurrence of melanoma cancer. Many of the lymph nodes under Mark's ear and in his neck had cancer. Major surgery was required to deal with the problem, not eardrops, as the first doctor had prescribed.

Perhaps a person is suffering from a physical problem such as a headache. A person who has a headache doesn't need healing of memories. He or she needs headache medicine. It would be ludicrous to take someone through a counseling session for healing of memories simply because the person had a headache. Such treatment would definitely be the wrong remedy for the problem. However, if the person experiences excruciating headaches every time he or she contemplates a deep hurt experienced in life, headache medicine is not the appropriate corrective for the problem.

Such medicine only focuses on removing the physical manifestation—the physical pain—and does not deal with the root cause—the recurring emotional pain. To deal with the root cause, the person must bring the past hurt to the surface and allow Jesus as Healer to minister to him or her and heal the hurt. When that has happened, the root of the problem will have been dealt with and the headaches will most likely stop.

I don't mean to imply that every physical ailment is the outworking of some deep-rooted problem. It is not. But since some physical ailments are related to some deeper problem, we need the discerning power of the Holy Spirit to guide us. Often we are like icebergs: our top ten percent may appear fine to everyone around us, but underneath we have much undealt-with emotional pain. If we are to be free, if we are to have victory, if we are to truly know God as our Father, we must deal with the pain.

We talked about the need for the right diagnosis of a problem and drew a parallel with what a doctor does when we are sick. Making the right diagnosis of our problem may well require the services of a trained Christian counselor. Often our past hurtful experiences have been buried deep within our subconscious. We may not even be aware of their presence, but nonetheless they are there, wreaking havoc in various areas of our life. Often, despite our best efforts to subdue them, the effects of these hurts continue unchecked, leading us to feelings of defeat and condemnation—all because we applied the wrong cure because we didn't understand the real source of the problem. This is where a trained counselor can help. As the counselor asks probing questions and listens to our answers, in time he or she can pinpoint the source of our problem. Having found the source of the problem, the counselor can then help us bring it to the surface where it can be properly dealt with. This process may take time and may be emotionally painful as we face situations in our life that we've buried in our subconscious and tried to hide from ourselves and others. But if we are determined to deal with the problem, investing our time and enduring the pain will pay off. We will find the freedom we seek.

Freedom is found only in Jesus. He is our Redeemer, our Sanctifier, our Healer, and our Deliverer. The situations we have encountered in life that hold us back from truly loving and accepting God as our Father must be brought before Jesus, who can deal with them and make us whole. Whether we do this with the help of a Christian counselor or do it on our own, the aim is always to bring the situation before Jesus. His touch brings redemption. His touch brings sanctification. His touch brings healing. His touch brings deliverance. His touch brings freedom and wholeness.

## Personal Application Points

1) Are there areas in your life that you have unsuccessfully struggled with to gain victory over?

2) Have you ever considered that the situation you struggle with could be the outward manifestation of a deeper problem?

3) Have you considered spending some time talking your problem over with a trained Christian counselor?

Chapter Eleven

# *GETTING TO*
# *KNOW GOD BETTER*

*H*aving overcome our misconceptions about God and having found freedom from past hurts that have held us back, we are now ready to get to know God better.

Any intimate relationship between two people—be it a child and his or her parent or a husband and wife—is a growing relationship and takes time to cultivate and develop. The more time we spend with the other person, the more we learn about the person and the more our love and respect for the person grow. To be a successful growing relationship, an intimate relationship requires work, commitment, and sacrifice on the part of both parties. Both parties must choose to spend time with the other person, even when they are busy or don't really feel like it. They must also be willing to change. A committed relationship requires that as people learn more about each other, they begin to make changes in their behavior that they may not be comfortable with, but such changes strengthen the relationship. A committed relationship means that people do not abandon each other even when things aren't going well.

Another important aspect of a good relationship is that the more time you spend with the other person, the more time you want to spend with the person. It is the same in our relationship with God.

## SEVEN STEPS FOR GETTING TO KNOW GOD BETTER

### Establish a Specific Place To Be Alone with God in Prayer

David, Moses, and Jesus all regularly went out into the beauty of nature to spend time with God. "But Jesus often withdrew to lonely places and prayed" (Luke 5:16). In Matthew 6:6, Jesus tells us, "When you pray [not *if* you pray, but *when* you pray], go into your room, close the door and pray to your Father, who is unseen." Your place of prayer could be a bedroom, kitchen, office, lounge, even a favorite spot outdoors. The actual location of the place is not as important as having a place where you can be alone and free from interruptions.

It is important to be alone with God in an environment free from interruptions because that is where real intimacy with God can be developed. True intimacy in a relationship cannot be accomplished in public. Instead, the couple must retreat to a place where they can be alone together uninterrupted. In such a place, the couple can be truly open and intimate with each other. If we want intimacy in our relationship with God, we must find a place where we can be alone with Him.

Having established the place in which to be alone with God, you can do some practical things to make the place as comfortable and conducive as possible to praying and communing with God. Some of the best times of communicating and being with my wife are when I'm comfortably curled up on the couch beside her. In that relaxed position, I begin to share openly and freely with her. One's relationship with God should be no different. Thus, having a place conducive to free and open conversation with God in prayer is essential. Unfortunately, many people mistakenly think that the only way to have quality time with God is on their knees on a cold floor at 6 A.M. Nothing is further from the truth. There may be times in our relationship with God when we just want to kneel humbly before Him. Most often, though, the more comfortable and relaxed we are, the easier and more naturally our time with Him will flow. The easier and more naturally our time together flows, the more we will enjoy and look forward to such times on a regular basis.

Atmosphere and surroundings play an important part in making a place conducive to good communication. A nice candlelit restaurant with soft music and comfortable overstuffed chairs is far more conducive to good communication between people than McDonalds or Burger King.

Often we think the place where we pray should be stark and bare like a courtroom where we come to meet God our judge, as though He were about to pass sentence on us. Such a notion is simply not true. When we go to our place of prayer we are going to spend time with God our Father, our Daddy, our Friend, our Lover, our Shepherd. Some practical things we can do to ensure that our place of prayer is comfortable and conducive to good communication with God are to have a comfortable chair to sit on or curl up in, furnish the space with some plants or flowers, pin on the wall a map of the world and some photos of people you're praying for to help you fix your mind on them as you pray. If you are in a place where you're likely to be interrupted, have a "Please Do Not Disturb" sign and hang on the door.

An intimate relationship with God, as already noted, is very personal and should be conducted in a place where you are not likely to be disturbed and where you are comfortable and able to let down your guard and share freely, openly, and easily with your heavenly Father.

## Make and Keep All
## Your Appointments With God

We will never develop a deep and intimate relationship with the Lord without a commitment to spending time with Him. To assure our spending time with Him, it's a good idea to have a set time each day. Just as I get to know my wife better through spending time with her and listening to how she feels about things, I get to know God better by giving Him my time and attention. When I make an appointment to spend time with my wife, I'm diligent to keep the appointment. If I were to fail to keep the appointment through carelessness or lack of desire, in essence I would be saying to her that other things are as important to me as she is or more important to me than she is. We say exactly the same thing to God when we fail to keep our appointments with Him.

Western society has become ensnared in a mesh of busyness. People seem to be frantically rushing from one activity to the next and then on to another. In the face of this frenzy, people experience a tragic dislocation and breakdown of their relationships with other people. They place career, making money, and a myriad of other concerns ahead of their personal relationships. The consequences of such choices are dire, as evidenced by the soaring divorce and suicide rates in America. (In fact, the divorce rate among

Christians is higher than that of the rest of American society.)

A similar dislocation is taking place today in American churches. Although pastors have never been busier and people are more involved in all manner of church programs, many churchgoers do not know God. Christians in America have lost the art of intimacy with their heavenly Father. They have carried over into their relationship with God the frantic activity that marks the rest of their daily lives. When they find themselves running out of time in their schedule, they begin crossing off the less important things to make room for all their other activities. All too often, the first thing to be scratched is their daily time with the Lord. Such action grieves God and sends a person's life into a tailspin, leading to spiritual divorce. In fact, placing God first on your list of things to do will assure you that everything else will get done. That's how God works.

"But if from there you seek the LORD your God, you will find him if you look for him with all your heart and with all your soul" (Deuteronomy 4:29). God promises blessings if we are true to His word. If we are serious about our relationship with God, we need to give God some of our "primetime." Making and keeping appointments with Him can result in a life of blessed, purpose-filled intimacy with the creator of the universe, and nothing is too great a sacrifice for such a blessing.

## Cultivate a Life
## Attitude of Praise to God

A life of praise is indispensable to knowing God. Cultivating such a life involves far more than dropping a few praise explicatives into our speech, replacing the periods with a "Praise God," as many are in the habit of doing. Real praise has to do with telling God the truth about Himself. This means that "praise God" is the opening of the statement, not the complete sentence itself or the sentence's punctuation. Our sentences should go more like this: "Praise God, for He is perfect and true, He cares for me daily." As we enter into praise in this way and begin to tell God the truth about Himself, He comes and inhabits our praises.

We may feel led to praise God in any number of ways, from more traditional forms such as speaking words of praise and singing hymns and scriptural choruses to less conventional means such as shouting to the Lord, dancing before Him, reading Scripture aloud to Him, and playing musical instruments to Him.

While there are countless ways to praise the Lord, we should remember that praise is a very personal thing. Our praise can be more meaningful if we express it in our own individual style. By using a personal form of praise, we are truly expressing ourselves to the Lord. Praise is not something to work ourselves into. It should come naturally. We shouldn't have to grit our teeth and say we're going to praise God today by singing to Him when we don't feel comfortable singing. If we're tone deaf and embarrassed to sing aloud to the Lord, we might want to praise God in a way that better suits our personality and our abilities.

Many Christians have, I'm sure, been at a church service where the worship leader has said said something like, "Let's all lift our hands and praise the Lord together as we sing." But those who find it difficult to raise their hands in public, may find their minds shifting from praising God to feeling embarrassed. They half-heartedly raise their hands, but only to stave off the greater embarrassment of not having them raised when everyone around them has their hands raised. Their hands may be raised, and from the outside they may look as though they're praising God, but inside they're overtaken with embarrassment and they're hanging on for the song to end so they can put their arms down and feel comfortable again. People often feel uncomfortable and embarrassed in such a situation because someone has manipulated them into praising God in a way they're not comfortable with. But this is not praise. It's the worship leader projecting onto people the way he feels comfortable praising God.

Since praise is a very personal expression, people must discover the ways in which they feel most comfortable praising God. Such ways should be an outgrowth of their personality and a full expression to the Lord of their praise and thanks for who He is and the many things He does for them daily. People who are musical might want to sing or play an instrument during their personal times of praise and worship to the Lord. God reads the thoughts and intents of our heart, and He knows what motivates us to sing or play our instrument to Him. The same is true of dancing and other forms of expression. God sees us expressing ourselves to the Lord, and however we feel led to praise Him is pleasing to God.

Nothing in the world makes me happier than when my wife says, "Honey, I want you to know that you're the neatest man in the world. Nobody else I know would so diligently take the garbage out the way you do every morning. You know I hate that job, and you just go and do it every morning without being asked. I love you for that." Now it's just a small thing she has praised me for, but for a while I walk around the house feeling ten feet tall. Every one of us needs that kind of praise, and when we receive it, we're drawn closer in relationship to the person who gave it.

God loves us and continually does things for us. Occasionally what He does may be big and miraculous, but most often the things He does are small things that we hardly notice. Regardless of whether it's a small thing or a large thing, God wants to hear us praise Him for it. He longs to hear us say, "I thank you and I praise you Father for taking care of me by doing *(whatever it is He has done for you)*. You know me better than I know myself. I love you and I worship you. You alone are worthy of all praise and honor." When He hears our praise and thanksgiving, He moves closer to us, and our intimate relationship with Him deepens.

### Be in Prayer at All Times

We are reminded throughout the New Testament to constantly talk to God in prayer: "And pray in the Spirit on all occasions" (Ephesians 6:18), "...pray continually" (1 Thessalonians 5:17), "...devote yourselves to prayer" (1 Corinthians 7:5). Develop the habit of being continually in prayer. Pray is not to be restricted just to mornings or evenings. We are to be in prayer all day long. I would have a very strange relationship with my wife if I spoke to her only in the morning when I got up or in the evening before I went to bed and ignored her throughout the rest of the day. So it is a strange relationship with God if we speak to Him only in the morning before we have crawl out of bed or in the evening before we drift off to sleep. Such a relationship has no chance of developing the type of intimacy we've been talking about in this book. A good relationship requires good communication. Ask any married couple who enjoy a close intimate relationship with each other, and they will tell you that good communication—being able to articulate their thoughts and feelings to each other—is the key to a successful relationship.

Talk to God all day long. Tell Him what you're feeling, ask for His help in difficult situations, tell Him how much you appreciate and love Him.

Communicating constantly with God is the life-blood of our relationship with Him.

## We Must Let God Speak to Us

For God to speak to us presupposes that we are listening for his voice. In John 10:4, Jesus tells us that His sheep know His voice. Jeremiah 33:3 says, "Call to me and I will answer you." These verses are talking about two-way communication with God—we speak, and God answers. For too many Christians today, communication with God has become one-way communication. They send a constant babel of prayer requests to God but do not listen for the answers to the very things they have asked Him about. So they become bewildered about why God never seems to answer their prayers. Finally they become bitter and disillusioned and say, "God doesn't care about me. He never answers my prayers."

Of course, God may very well have answered their prayers; the answer may have been "No" "Wait." People blame God for not answering them when all the while they haven't been listening for Him to speak to them. It's like calling someone on the phone and asking a lot of questions, then hanging up before the person has a chance to answer. It's ludicrous, but it's exactly what many Christians do. As a result, these people become broken and bitter, and some leave the faith claiming that God is not real and doesn't speak to people today. Sadly, they miss God's voice simply because they weren't listening for it.

Listening for God's voice presupposes people will recognize it when they hear it. I never cease to be amazed by the number of people who think they have heard God speak to them but are not quite sure. Perhaps the biggest holdup to people who are seeking God's will for their lives is that they can't recognize His voice when He speaks to them. They think they've heard His voice and often spend months seeking confirmation that it was indeed God who spoke to them. It would be so much easier for them if they knew God's voice and recognized it the moment He spoke.

I used to take part in a Saturday morning Christian radio program in Salem, Oregon, where I live. One day I was on an airplane flying across the country when a woman, whom I had never seen before, turned around and said, "I know that voice, you're Duane Rawlins aren't you?" I nodded, and she went on to tell me how she listened to me on the radio every Saturday morning. She identified me by my voice. She knew what my voice sounded like, since she had listened to it week after week on the radio and was able to recognize me the moment I spoke. Can we recognize God's voice like that? Do we hear His voice daily? There is no easy way to learn to recognize His voice other than by spending time with God and learning to discern when He is speaking to us so that we will recognize it when He speaks in the future.

I have some friends who lived for a time in the tiny Kingdom of Tonga in the South Pacific. Tonga is a long way from anywhere, and my friends liked to sit down in the evening and listen to the news that came by shortwave radio from the BBC in London. Unfortunately, there were a number of shortwave stations gathered around the same spot on the radio dial. My friends had to tune their radio very carefully to make sure they had it right on the spot where they could hear the BBC. The slightest turn of the dial too much to the left or to the right and they would lose the BBC news bulletin they were listening to and instead would hear Radio Moscow's English station or some station where someone was speaking a language they couldn't understand.

As with the shortwave radio, we can easily tune God out. Most often we don't deliberately tune Him out. Other things seem to divert our attention, however, and before long we're not hearing the voice of the Lord speaking to us. One touch of the dial is all it takes to tune God out. We must be diligent that we keep God tuned in, since a one-way conversation is no conversation at all, and a one-way relationship is no relationship at all. Intimate fellowship with God is a two-way thing—we must not just talk to Him but must listen for Him so that we can hear Him speak to us.

### Study the Bible Daily

"For the word of God is living and active" (Hebrews 4:12). "In the beginning was the Word, and the Word was with God, and the Word was

God" (John 1:1). The Bible is God's Word to us, and God inhabits His Word. As we study His word, read it, and absorb it, God begins to open our eyes to who He really is. We begin to see new things about God every time we open the Bible. The Bible is vibrant and alive, full of insight and understanding into the beauty and wonder of God. It is a record of God's patient, loving dealings with mankind, and as we read this record, the full character of God is wondrously demonstrated for us. The Bible is our "knowing God" textbook, and it is impossible to truly know God in an intimate way without knowing His Word. If we want to know God, we must become men and women of His Word.

There is another aspect of studying God's Word. Not only do we learn about who God is, but as we study the Bible, God begins to speak to us through it. As you study His word, God may speak a passage of scripture into our life, saying this is for you, read it, and apply it to your life. This is one of the ways in which God speaks to us. Since God sometimes uses passages from the Bible as His voice, we need to read and study the Bible daily and listen for His voice as we read.

### Get Involved in Praying for and Meeting the Needs of Others

"[F]ar be it from me that I should sin against the LORD by failing to pray for you," declares the prophet Samuel in 1 Samuel 12:23. An intimate relationship with God is not to be a selfish, self-centered relationship where we block out others and claim God for ourselves. God is an outward-looking God who not only created human beings but also loves every person who has ever been, is presently, or will ever be alive. God uses us to express practically His love and concern for people. People are His arms and legs on the world. As individuals and as the church, we are the practical representation of the body of Christ to all the earth. We are surrounded by people with needs—needs that God wants to meet. And to meet them, God wants to use us.

The first step in the process is to take the needs of another to the Lord in prayer. As you pray, ask God to share with you His heart feelings for the person and show you practical ways to minister to that person. Listen to what the Lord tells you, and then do what He asks.

You may be wondering what this has to do with having intimacy with God. The motivation and desire to want to pray for and reach out to those with needs come from our relationship with the Lord. As we get closer to God, we learn that His heart aches for both the spiritually and the physically needy. If we are striving to please God, our heart will ache for the spiritually and physically needy people around us as well. In our times together with the Lord, we should be concocting plans and schemes to help meet people's needs. Nothing brings more joy, more fulfillment, and more excitement to us than the look on the face of someone whom we have helped in the Lord's name. We then take back that joy, that fulfillment, and that excitement to our relationship with God, which becomes deeper and more intimate as a result.

After several years of meditating upon God's Word, God began to challenge me about the importance of caring for the poor, the needy, widows, orphans, and those coming out of prison. Time after time, the Lord brought my attention back to James 1:27, which says, "religion that God accepts as pure and faultless is this: to look after orphans and widows in their distress and to keep oneself from being polluted by the world." As a result, my wife and I established New Life Ministries, which provides a preschool for children and a half-way house for women coming out of prison who had accepted Jesus while they were still incarcerated.

This ministry has added new dimensions to my relationship with the Lord. I have begun to grasp in greater depth God's heart for the poor and the needy. Perhaps God will stir you towards ministering to the needs of others. If He does, pour yourself into it, drawing on His strength as you minister to people. As you do God's work, you will discover that your knowledge, understanding, and experience of God has grown immensely.

## CONCLUSION

God is our heavenly Father. He wants us to know him as a father. Scripture reveals God's character as our Father, and Jesus provided a living example of His Father's heart. Now it is time for us to do our part. We must move closer to God our Father. This, as we have seen, is not always easy to do. We carry childhood hurts and scars that can hinder our entering into the kind of relationship God wants to have with us. The ball is now in our court, however, and we must make the next move. It's up to us to decide to deal with those things that hold us back. I have found that if we will take the first few faltering steps towards God, He will move closer to us. If we are willing to expose those things that keep us from knowing Him as our Father, He will deal with them. God's heart aches to know us and love us as a Father love his children. But God will not force Himself upon us. We must choose Him. He waits longingly for us to choose Him and to relate to Him as our heavenly Father.

## Personal Application Points

1) Are there any areas discussed in this chapter where you feel your relationship with God is weak?

2) What are some practical steps you can take to strengthen these areas?

3) What is the most valuable insight you have gained through reading this book? How are you going to apply that insight to your life?